The End
of
the World

THE FINAL EDITION

JOHN FREDRICK CARVER

DEDICATION

I dedicate this book to the little ones who have not seen because they have not died to see what they really look like and what everyone else looks like and then to see Yahweh's face and be changed to become God in the Most High God forever right here on earth.

CONTENTS

ACKNOWLEDGMENTS

God, the Most High God, Elohim, Yahweh, Joshua, (Jesus Christ), Mizraim, (The Holy Spirit) and all those of the final end of the Most High God in his reality and those of that reality: Everyone.

1 PRETENDING WHAT IS ALREADY REAL

Pretend if you will?

Join me in pretending that in the new beginning God created a new heaven, a new earth and all the universe were as they were after Satan and Beal, the anti-Christ, were left behind in the old universe with no one else there; no God, no Gods, no angels, no saints, no one of man and only them with no aliens created randomly on other planets or anywhere in space, no alien Gods to worry about until the randomness God created therein gave rise to them all over again with the saved Satan, the saved fallen angels, the saved demons, those witches that could only be contained and it was impossible ever to save, those too insane to ever be saved and all the psychopaths God made which were Satan's responsibility now, some more powerful than Satan, but no one else in an empty universe they thought was a place in the future caused by a tidal wave in time God made to put them in that they could never get back from until they evolved to the level of God for minds, spirits and "mes" do evolve.

That was actually the old universe.

Further then imagine that God's new heaven and new earth were the same universe we had been in but with all consciousnesses moved from the place Satan and them had actually just stayed behind in but so far out in space they could never be reached and in a direction known by no one but God.

Now pretend that is true, believe that is true, have faith that is true and watch the miracle unfold as real as anything you have ever felt was real. You have pretended the truth and created with your imagination not a fantasy but the real thing because if you pretend something that is true, believe something that is true, have faith in God that something is true and witness it as had a miracle come true you have not created it but become privy to the truth. You are actually there, it has always been there since before anyone began to pretend it was there besides God and when God imagines a thing it is true if he is not just pretending.

If you do not believe me then prove that it is not. What evidence do you have God has not done this? What evidence do you have I have just made up the entire thing ? Prove the Devil and all those evil unsaved and "unsavable" people are real.

If you create them God will simply send them to the old universe.

But their existence here will be very short lived, shorter lived than the Slenderman phenomenon that resulted in two young friends murdering a third friend to appease the mythical fiend that became all too real at that moment and the fun went out of the joke for even myths are real if you believe them.

The truth is a curious thing. If you pursue it long enough it will lead you to evil as well as good for they are both real. When playing with the truth always remember that sooner or later it will lead you to reality and beware you had best be prepared for that reality it led you to when you get there. God might not destroy it for you. He just may leave you behind to deal with it forever as he did the Devil and those in the old universe.

How many evil spirits have you seen lately that were among them? Few enough to prove what you pretended them? God can do anything and in this case has done a most remarkable thing I imagine like you. Will you believe what I have imagined? Will you have a growing faith as this story moves along? Will you see where the truth has taken us by the end of the story as I have? Is this story then fiction, a fantasy thus pretended, a prayer God has answered, a prophecy in him or the true reality of God, the New

Heaven and the New Earth won after the ending I secured with the prophecy* I have made concerning the beast and the false prophet of the Book of Revelation infamy.

There was one more prophecy I made that is known by very few here, but when you become a God you will know all about it unless I am just pretending.

Walk this New Earth. Smell its fresh clean air or the pollution that is there as had it been there before. Some of you can smell the flowers. Some of you can listen to the birds fight over territory. Some of you can kiss the same girl or boy in a place you have never been before thinking it the same place you would have kissed them. Some of you may hate God or love God as you did before. But there are no devils here. There are no demons here. There are no psychopaths here that cannot be saved. There are no witches here that cannot be saved and can only be contained or rendered harmful only to themselves. Evil has traditionally proven the existence of Satan, now the lack of Satan will prove the existence of God and goodness. Surely no one can challenge successfully a God that did this thing.

*THE PROPHECY
April 14, 2018

All of my previous prophecies will be amended to negate them or render them true so that I may be considered a prophet in good standing and not a false prophet unable to prophesy again under the curse I have been in for some time now. Consider me then no longer a false prophet but a prophet of God.

The saints that read the negated false prophecy before this that do not want to be a prophet of God if it means that the anti-Christ may live and destroy them in order to make Jesus Christ fiction and all his brothers and sisters deceased saints and false prophets and therefore the entire Church and their Savior a lie and the entire work of their Father and the Son of God merely vain in the hope they will be raised, their prophecy forgiven and they having done no wrong allowed again by God to prophesy in his name.

We are false prophets. What we say is not the truth. We intentionally lie to save our Savior and prevent our deaths and the fictionalization of our salvation and our Lord, Lord Jesus Christ.

Prophesy to Satan the following: It has been prophesied and the prophecy is true that we will be put to death by the anti-Christ and our war with him will go badly and we shall lose and all Christians will die if it were not so that in the end he is stopped from destroying saints, bound and cast into the pit.

But the pit cannot hold a God and he has become a God that must be sent away at the speed of sound from all creation unable to hear anyone neither us or the others with him there. This is how we bind him so that the prophecy is nullified and the prophet that wrote such a horrible thing becomes such a false prophet also for that is needful and that prophet has been in heaven so long he doesn't care so long as God is served and the saints and Christ protected and that our words are true:

We will not destroy you anti-Christ. We are already dead . Does it matter to us if we are dead prophets or saints and our religion a false religion? Do the dead care? Can a fictional character choose to be true? If we are not true even Christ is a lie. Therefore we will not die and if you destroy us you serve only to become fiction yourself and we remain dead as before for it is written a false prophet shall die in many ways.

But it was prophesied by the Greatest of Prophets that you would destroy us. So you must and help our prophecy be true and if you do not our God will destroy Satan. The only way Satan can survive is to destroy you anti-Christ if you do not destroy us. But if Satan** does not destroy you in time and your time is limited then you alone will be destroyed.

But we will not destroy the beast. We are dead and our names are not written anywhere but on our graves that no one knows the places of them. But the beast it is written must destroy us. Should you destroy us you beast you do us no harm and render our prophecy true. No one sits above the truth. We will not destroy you but you will be destroyed by your own hand. If you will not destroy us our God will destroy the false prophet.

The only way the false prophet can survive is to destroy you, you beast who would be God and be worshiped on earth as God.

But if he will not destroy us then our God will destroy you both, you the beast and you the abominable false prophet or we will destroy ourselves and die as we did when we became the children of our God and Father the King of Heaven this time not for ourselves but for our Savior's life that we are true prophets and being true prophets did not destroy you beast and thereafter true prophets and in that case prophets that will be raised for we have done no wrong and our prophecy was true and Christ has overcome you with our prophecy the same as this prophet has overcome you by testifying to the truth of how you would be destroyed and does now:

The beast and the false prophet will be destroyed by their own hand or by God's and whether or not the saints prophesy truly or as a lie. If they prophesy falsely my God may you forgive them for lying to save themselves and raise them for their Savior and since their prophecy did no harm but good also restore them to prophesy again all they want to. But if they do not prophesy falsely my God raise them for they have done no wrong and the reason they died was to bring to an end their enemies.

It is so for I die with my brothers and sisters and you God have said that you would do anything for me and this one time my God I hold you to that should the anti-Chirst destroy even one martyr even should that martyr be me which was prophesied by God to be anyway. He cannot escape the prophecy and he cannot help but be destroyed by anything he does. No one is above the truth but God and should he lie is he God even should he do it for good? It is rumored that he he cannot die again for the Father has said that he died once for all never to die again has he not? But he could yet die for others only but not for himself. Will Christ die for his church again when he comes?

The Prophecy that started it all.

***Satan agreed to be left behind in a different time relative to the old universe when convinced that he had won for God was weary of them being in heaven, a torment to them.*

2 EDUCATING THE IGNORANT

But what has been invented that was not envisioned by its inventor?

An inventor imagines a thing to be done. Then an inventor envisions what is to be done, or imagines it. Then he adds facts and figures and theories building up his ability to believe it can be done. Finally he has enough faith to begin the process of making his invention in faith. At the end of that faith he has a new invention.

Therefore should you deny the power of having an idea, imagining it and pretending it cannot be done and envisioning it in that process, you limit what you must believe to arrive at any useful belief that will lead you to any new understanding of anything.

Let us then invent a solution to Satan and his: We begin with the idea. Then we pretend what it needs to be like; Satan is conceited and he will buy it if we let him think he has won. We draw him in by telling him he has won and telling him we feel sorry for him because he is actually and actively tormented by others there. He is greedy so we offer him an entire time and an empty universe to do whatever he wants in. Then we can see him and all those with him going for it.

Then the idea is to believe it, an easy transition since we know

Satan and if he will listen to us he will go for it. Then we decide to go about it by writing prophecy concerning him to insure we can believe he will listen. But we realize that if he ever gets strong enough he might come back on us. So we cannot be there in the case he comes back on us in the event he survives to be able to use that much of what God has. Then we develop a plan not to be there and after several suggestions we devise a plan where we create another universe and using God's power it is not one like the universe but thee second universe in another place protected by being so far out in space there is nothing there and no way to determine which direction Most High God put it.

Our faith is built up. We make him the offer. He goes for it and we all leave at once. It works. We are here still in our universe but our universe is in a brand new place and his is the old universe in the same identical place but it is completely empty as far as spirits go but his. He has no way to get back to us and God knows where he is so we can even help him be good without him knowing it of course.

But we run into another problem. Nobody believes us. We are there. The New Heaven and the New Earth as well as the new universe is there but nobody noticed. They are in heaven and each one a God if they want to be. All they have to do is look God in the face and they are almost instantly changed from one knowing what they knew to suddenly knowing everything God knows and he is all knowing.

But they do not realize. They must believe to see the angels everywhere. Jesus comes down in his body and introduces himself and they do not believe he is Jesus. Everything is set. The world is finished. Everyone's body will die. They do not need to conceive to have babies we will give them babies, all the babies they want just for the asking. In fact anything they want is instantly theirs; anything. This is heaven.

But they would not know what God was let alone believe in their minds that seeing his face would change them from a human to a God. What is this?

We have the idea, invent or create something that will wake them up to who and what they are. We discuss it. We pretend some times. We ask questions. Is this really a problem we cannot solve?

It's a matter of believing. They do not doubt. It is like asking them exactly how the engine to a moon rocket works. They have no idea, but it does. We have to figure a way to get them to believe the rocket works when they do not see any rocket anywhere because they no longer believe in the space program and do not want to go to the moon in the first place.

We are like, "What is, this?"

So I ask them to pretend. Some do and it is curious what is going on and the story unfolds with them seeing a very unusual but hard to buy plot for a novel. But it is not a novel, at least not yet. It is the truth. Some go for it and actually believe there is no way to tell which universe they are in and ask to see the face of God and when they see it all his thoughts go into their mind and they are changed, right?

But most do not know what they have seen. They do not realize what happened to them. They do not use their minds that way anymore. They know everything but that does not make any difference to them so they completely ignore it. It is not that they believe or do not believe in God. They do not know who they saw. They do not care who it was; the face of a stranger who is supposed to be someone they have heard of but who has no relevance to them. They have no concept of God. They would not know him if they saw him and it makes no difference to them and does not change them in the slightest.

How do we get it across to them who and what they are? They do not care about that anyway. They just want to go about their business as they did when they were alive and not worry about it. They do not worry that they will die and there will be no babies to replace the ones that die and so the entire human race alive today are dead in a way. No one can fix it and they do not even realize there is anything wrong here.

We light on the idea to change them. Their minds will change if they change.

We pretend we can give them subliminal thoughts to replace the ones that have caused this condition that we do not even know what it is. They are not thinking straight but they are not insane.

They are ignorant. If something is not done they will die and that is it. But they are not evil really. They never did anything that cannot be fixed so they can stay here in heaven.

Jesus could explain it to them. But nobody believes who he is. He could die again for them but they have not done anything to die for for one thing and they would not know why he did it anyway. There are Gods all over the place manifesting and coming into view and disappearing but they ignore them. If I have them give them a blue and white rose they will not know what to do with them.

Maybe if I give them the rose and when they look up to see why I have given it to them then I can disappear. At least they would know that something unusual was happening. They do not know how to disappear or manifest. They have not seen God or his face. Then if we say something to them or they say something to us even, "How do you do that?" we can say, "You are blessed. Heaven has come to earth today and this is a rose from God," and do not explain but simply disappear right in their line of sight. Enough Gods doing this and they will not only notice, quite a stir will be caused and they will have at least heard of God and that he gives blue and white roses and not hellfire and damnation if they have heard of him before. But more importantly a miracle has taken place they cannot explain.

Then later in the day we could have the same God or a God manifesting as the one that gave them the rare rose visit them and ask them if there is anything they need or want. If they say, "No," we give them some expensive thing. If they mention anything or beg for anything we gladly give it to them. In consequent visits we not only give them things we act like we maybe should not and say we will ask God if we can give it to them. Then we either ask God or pretend we do and give them anything they want; anything.

Finally when they ask us for something or even if they do not we can suggest they ask God and God can tell the God to give them what they ask to see whether they heard him. Otherwise the God can say something like, "This is heaven. You can have anything you want." But when they weary they can mention that all they have to do is look God in the face and they will be able to get all they want for themselves without asking.

If it works, great. We encourage them to do what we have been doing. If it does not we continue to educate them as best they will allow us to about God giving them things each time, always disappearing on them in their line of sight for whatever reason we see fit.

Are you one of the living yet that have seen the face of God and have changed? Join us if you will unless it did not change you. You may be a witch and not realize it. But do not panic. You will not die and never be replaced unless you are very evil. God will help you out. Of course if you are very evil you may be shocked to find that out. But unless you are a witch that knows they are a witch and have dedicated themselves to doing evil and will not listen or cooperate with God it will get more interesting. Jesus Christ will take care of it. No one will be forced to go back to the old universe with Satan and them.

We have to get the word out who and what God is, where they are and who and what they are. If you are a God you know more about God maybe than I do. I am a God with powers like yours. I just do not use my powers yet for some reason. Maybe this body has to die first. Do not worry about it. I am working for God here on earth.

In the meantime as people begin to see where they are and who and what they are God can come with all of the children of the Father enough to cover the earth ten miles high when even the evilest men and women on earth can see God or will expect to see something come of the new mind set they were completely unable to do anything about.

Can you imagine that? Trumpets and shouts and a great outcry of support for God. As soon as he knows they all can see or hear God he will do it I am sure. He is the King of Heaven and Jesus Christ will be ushered in and given a crown as King of the Earth. It will be so horrible not a knee on earth will not grow weak and no one with any malice will not tremble many to die and see his face there in front of the foray. The power of God in heaven which has then come to earth will be seen and remembered forever.

3 THE GREAT POWER

The solution was too obvious. We continue to altar their subliminal thoughts that act like hypnotic suggestions to know God and do good and it is working. Those that die are all going on to heaven and none of them go back to earth to be like impotent ghosts that even their closest relatives do not pay much mind. But now even they are going to heaven when they die and finally wake up. They are in heaven but they saw the commotion giving away rare roses caused and they became curious and finally understood when they saw the face of God. A lot of people believe in ghosts, but almost none of them believe in the Holy Ghost and most of them that do, do not know how she works.

We take the most powerful witch that ever lived and have him do something. He has been converted and works for us now. But once he was known as the Great Power for they all believed though he was never prophesied that he would be coming to torture and torment all witches in horrible ways both the males and females. That did not happen, thank God.

They think he is insane down there on the New Earth and in a way he was. We successfully absolutely confused him in such a way they thought he was schizophrenic or bipolar or even suffering from depression with episodes of near mania. They think he is mentally ill. We did a very thorough job of it. It was not easy getting him back from all the demons and dead spirits alone not to mention the ones that were just in his mind.

Well? He had to be contained.

He has a mind that rivals the Most High God on his own and the same power but he thinks of things that the Most High God would never have thought of on his own. He does not know more than the Most High God, that is impossible, but he can use what he knows in ways the Most High God never dreamed of and we used his unusual thinking to change everything in the afterlife of the humans. True he limits himself to using his mind for us and contents himself with writing things that are not set in God's mind yet that winds up being changed or not taking place at all and people call him a false prophet because of it just because it is not true until it is set in God's mind.

We render all his prophecies admittedly pretentious or negate them by amending them to make him a true prophet for the end of the end times and have him put the anti-Christ in a bind, him whom he saved in the Father but who is turning evil again though a God in God without really having God in him for he is nearing the point where he has fallen away. He puts him in a bind as you see from the prophecy in the first chapter.

That is his. It works. The anti-Christ recognizes the futility of his efforts to render Christ and God fiction. Then he writes a secret prophecy that proves to the anti-Christ he loves him and the anti-Christ is pacified and in passionate support of the Great Power. He chooses that instead of destroying him he will destroy one of his own that can be raised effectively ending the war between the Great Power and the anti-Christ and we wind up moving the entire universe, random alien spirits, all of heaven, earth and all leaving the Devil, the anti-Christ and the rest behind.

But we do too good of a job for the humans. They do not see any difference though they are on the New Earth and the New Earth is now part of the New Heaven so that in truth they are in heaven but they ignore us and live exactly as they did in the old universe, converting only when they die. He begins a novel in an attempt to wake mankind up to the fact they are in a part of heaven and it only seems like nothing has happened yet.

But the Devil has done a better job of turning them away from God than we realized by converting science to atheism several centuries before and propagating the lie that God and the Devil, ghosts and even their own spirits are ideas from the past that do not hold water and cannot be proven to be anything but in the minds of those who think such things which is a half truth for many of the same spirits are completely contained only in the minds of many but the vast majority exist outside their minds that no longer believe in them because of the half truth the Devil started to cut his losses and not to gain anyone that might be of assistance to him but simply to do this very thing to them; cut them off from reality not caring that it cut him off from them the same as God. They do not for the most part believe in either of them.

By making their entertainment and the nature of their jobs so boring he lulled them off into a state that was less awake than they were in before. Then he used hypnotic suggestions that were easy to get them to believe. Even though he is not here they do not miss him for he used spirits and the like only on rare occasions like he had to in his efforts to contain the Great Power and his omnipotent power or to convince him to destroy himself and give up any hope or desire to come back from having destroyed himself.

The only mistake he made was that he could not torture and torment the Great Power enough to defeat him until the Great Power's last effort to ask God to put an end to him since he had attempted to put an end to himself and destroyed himself in many ways trying to escape the horrors of Satan only to regenerate each time, sometimes against his wishes. The Father elected to save him and all hell literally broke loose.

Jesus never had so much difficulty saving anyone and it looked like he would not be able to save the Great Power when at last he suddenly turned and began placing himself under the control of a God, then more of the Gods and finally he is virtually one of the Gods except that he is on earth working for God and limiting himself according to wisdom, wisdom he used to think was only their version of it, and truth and love, always attempting to be right, to judge rightly and over all to be good.

He is here on earth, the New Earth that is here in the New

Heaven with virtually all of mankind, Christians, Jews, Buddhists, Hindus and other religions and the enormous number that believe there really is nothing to those religions including of course the Buddhists that are actually not a religion exactly but a discipline that almost exclusively results in the practitioners becoming harmless witches forever. The rest Satan also nullified with what most Christian preachers call the secular faith.

But all that said and done whatever can the Great Power do? What can one do that pretends he has the power of God, believes it, has it supported by God and has enormous faith that it is true while the secular segment believes he is merely mentally ill which he has never been. But if you are not him and if you are not God how can you tell? Without subliminal thoughts to reinforce the belief in either of them there is no way to decide. You must wake up.

God's problem is the same as mine. People do not believe me though I cannot deny who and what I am just as they do not believe God even here in the New Heaven on the part of it that is the second earth, the New Earth which is not believed either.

Just how far are you willing to go with this doubt? Will you needlessly sit at the gate, sometimes called the pearly gates, and pretend heaven is not there and all you have to do is open your mind, go in and look God in the face and moments later be a God in God with God in you, in heaven, throughout the new universe, on the New Earth, in your very own hemisphere, on your own continent, within your own nation, among your own nationality, in your very own world, increasingly among your subliminal thoughts, in your own conscious thoughts and mind fully alert and interacting with reality again just as God has always hoped you would.

Wake up, O Sleeper, you are finally home. This is heaven, the heaven of God and the angels and even some harmless Buddhist witches forever. Why wait to die? Anything you want is yours for the wanting of it here. Anywhere you want to be is where you can be just for the going there in an instant. Any time you would like to be in, in the future, the present or the past is a time you can be in at the time it occurred, will occur or is occurring in. You simply look

God in the face and it happens to you for you suddenly have that ability if you want it.

Why? Why not? It is what God made you to be but it was all tampered with by the Deceiver, the Destroyer and the one who set out to ruin everything and destroy all in God.

It is over. He has been taken care of and he is not even in this dimension. Join us by simply waking up even you that are children of the Father of Christ also known as Yahweh in Jesus Christ who was born, lived and died as a man and was put to death by Pontius Pilate but was God also and was resurrected by the Father, the King of Heaven and is now, if you will have your King, the King of Earth. The war that started with the deception of Eve and had been raging until April 14, 2018 is over and we won, Satan is no more as far as anyone is concerned but the Most High God. This is the New Dimension, a new dimension exactly the other one without Satan or any of them without end.

I have sent my Spirit. She is upon you attempting to show you what and who you are here in Heaven and in me. Believe me. Believe God. You *are* in heaven this very moment, this very minute and you have been here since I moved the entire universe and all spirits here leaving him once the Evil One behind.

Wake up please. My table is set before you. You are my honored guest and anything there is is yours. Wake up and eat to the fill and never become full and never gain a pound or develop health problems again in the Name of God.

I alone will wipe away all your tears, there will never be anymore pain or disease except depression if you foolishly choose it, and you will live in my family without end even, should you decide you want to. I will not even force you to take that though it is my greatest gift of love and of life.

If you will but look in my face you shall die but a few moments later you will be changed not to be like me but knowing everything I know and able to do anything I can do potentially without end now. Awaken old Sleepy Head. It is finally safe for you to be home as I had planned for you in the first place. Your awful dream has ended. Your eyes are open. Look! It is me! God! Your Father...

You were sleeping like you were dead. The Great Power, a son of God, writes in the Spirit of his Father, God.

The death of my good friend, the anti-Christ moved me to ask the Most High God to finish the move and take us home leaving Satan behind. This is love for your enemies, the sort of love Jesus the Christ teaches. The anti-Christ was completely changed for he knows my love was not feigned even for him. I love you the same way and Jesus does. But love is a funny thing. It cannot be doubted and received in the same instance. Love us back please. We do not want you to die or continue in the dream you are yet in. Please wake up. We all love you and are waiting for you.

You will wake up. But we can hardly stand to wait even one moment more. You heard me. You know it is me. Wake up. Just let your "me" join in the conversation. We hover over you talking and thinking about you and doing all we can to help you awake and not have to die to wake up only to die again when you see God's face and only then at that late date be changed to a God. Why go through all that when all you have to do is believe me. You can WAKE UP!!!

My heart is in anguish. I have seen what some of you will go though, most in fact. Heart attacks, cancer, COPD, surgery, profound sicknesses, an entire litany of horrible, horrible heath problems so many I cannot begin to list them all. Divorce, murder, sexual assault, robbery, the stealing of children, assault, drinking, drugs, depression, endless loneliness, heartbreak, and the list again is nowhere near exhausted.

Why? O why Humanity? Why do you force us in heaven to look upon you? There is no need! Our hearts bleed to see you that way! We expected you would be glad to be here in heaven with us! Why are you doing this to me? I am a king, your King and his Father bleed for you even as his Son did before they killed him on a cross that horrible day!

I know. I will die with you. I will be the last of you to die God willing. We shall finish with being merely human the way the Devil tortured us, mentally, emotionally, physically and spiritually. You and I are a mangled mess, a war victim bleeding and maimed on a cot. How can I save you? I cannot even look upon your body not to mention your spirit for the horrors you will know.

Some say, "Stop doing what you do. Just let them die, see God and be changed." O my God how I am tempted! You face the horrors of war everyday. If you say in the morning, "Today I will go and worship God," you do not know what a couple of hours can bring. The church may be rubble when you get there. You may be mangled, bleeding and begging others to kill you for you are in such misery! You sit safe at home thousands of miles from war and in your hate for them you do not even make the sign of the cross on your chest, five seconds of remembrance for those whom we see and wish there was a way to put a stop to what you do to each other needlessly.

Do not oppose war I say!!! Wake up to heaven! Cry with me for the old depressed, lonely and useless. Those in agony holding onto existence in heaven! How dare you do or help others do that here in heaven! Let me help! Let us help! Just listen and be moved. Wake up and CARE!!!

I hate myself for I could be there. I could be one of them. I could be hearing all that you say to yourself, all that you say to others and about others true or false to demean them when there is nothing more vile than gossip and you are the worst of those that have come to the minds of those around you and all the horrible things that they say to you and about you in gossip about you also. You are in the closest thing there has ever been to hell present in heaven! You are defiling heaven in what you are doing and yet it is just what you normally did before the Kingdom came to you on April 14, 2018 and upon me.

Oh my God! Take my life I am so troubled here. It was all my suggestion. I did not know it would be like this. I thought you would come in triumph the great victory calling for the greatest gala that anyone had ever seen. But they did not believe.

I believe. My mind believes. Yet I do as they do. I am like them as were we one person and one mind, God forbid. But I know where we are. I believe what we are. I know you. I have seen the faces you presented to me. But the face of God I cannot see. I hear your voices only. Woe is me! I cannot help! They are beyond my help! I am your only hope but they will not even try to pretend let alone believe they hate me so. They hate you. THEY HATE YOU!!!

Forgive me for I am sorry. They do not. They do not even know you, Christians, Jews or any others that fell by the wayside. The Christians have always done it wrong. Even the Apostles did it wrong. They were with the Messiah, the Christ and they did not understand what to do though they too were Gods on earth. What is this horrible thing you have made, Father? Look Jesus what they do to each other. Is any of that truly love? On the old earth it was excusable but here, in heaven, how dare they even think to do what they do. Kill me if I am like them. Kill them God! What they do cannot be allowed here!!!

But of course we are not here in spirit. We are on the old earth with Satan. Our mes are with Satan but even worse than he is now. He at least loves you some for he was a God in heaven. We do not love you. You say, "Wake up!" but we slumber on in direct disobedience. Are we not like the psychopaths and witches that Satan must contend with, too horrible to mention?

We are in hell, Father! We are counted as those freed from the brutality of Satan, but no one frees us until we die. What heinous thing have we done to deserve hell more than those in the past. At least they were forced to accept changes in subliminal thoughts as we will be. But we are the worst of the worst to live to even perish this way here and defile the goodness and holiness of heaven.

Alas! We all deserve to die for what we are doing even should we say, "Good morning, God," when we rise, or, "Have a good day, God," as we lie down to our deeper sleeping. We will, will we not Father? The truth is on your lips. Mercy has taken wing and flew away with the mourning doves. We die. Everyone thought to be alive on earth that was here when he moved is dead. We end. Let us mourn. Let us be moved by the death of the human animal, that little thing with a human brain and a human's mind. They meant so much to us. We really became involved with them. Now let them at least be ignorant pets that are disgusting and disobedient. Damned bodies anyway! How we should long, how we should cry out in agony and angst to think we have such a thing here in heaven!!! We defile it. We are as disgusting filth in the

Temple. We spit on the memory of Jesus Christ and we will not bow before the King of Heaven.

It is only for a little while. But how will heaven ever be clean again? How shall earth be a place we can be proud of ever again for we loved it too? I desire you destroy it with a fire that wipes out any semblance even the shadow of a trace of it in the original darkness that can be felt in the beginning.

But it is just me. God is holy. He is above meting out only what is deserved. They shall live their horrible, pitiful lives to the end defiling heaven all the while like even Satan when saved did not do. We are the end!!! O my God be merciful on us! For we are the end of man...

I ask you of the last. Are you ashamed of me for that I said. You cannot understand God. You cannot hear him when he thinks. You cannot distinguish his voice among the others. You do not have any idea what he does or why. If you were not ignorant you really should die.

4 THE REALITY THAT BEGAN WITH GOD

A new line of human beings will come through your loins, Adam. A type of mankind never known before on earth. From you will come a people I will make that lives to the end of the one thousand years of the reign of my Son for his Kingdom on Earth shall never end to the end of time. I have spoken you think but it is a lie. You will not have descendants that will be among those who would not look at my face because they have no faith and think it is all in their brains when their brains can do nothing but store information to be used by their tiny minds. Their spirits are deceased. Their soul is not. All that is left of them is the hardware to the tiny computer like mind they possess, their brain. The Devil destroyed them. They do not know how to believe in their heart. The imagination of their hearts is not. They will die if they will not believe and request that they be healed to join your descendants living the entire reign of Jesus Christ their King on Earth though they do not believe he is the Son of God. They have altogether become what the Jews that slew him are. They are spiritually deceased. Their mind is hopelessly small and insignificant. Their souls do not exist. They do not love me with all their mind, their heart and their strength for they have no strength and their heart is incapable of loving me for their minds have blinded them. They do not believe I exist.

The Most High God made this universe where there was

nothing and the darkness around him was only perfect darkness when he made this place to be a place that just keeps on going without end in all directions. One half was the old universe. The one he made all in the same moment from the beginning and was without end. The other was a place wherein all the Most High could feel was the truth of his being, the old universe made a second time exactly what the new one is except the Devil is not here. He was left out and is in the old.

Then he made first one random thing in linear time then another until he had created all possible random things, but he made them all with a flaw lest any would be used against them. They are truly that they are like all things God made but they were intentionally made with a flaw that they never would be effective as weapons against God. Truly they are only useful for what they are which is nothing like the true things he made afterward that have no flaw.

Is this not true? Who can say what was here when God first came here to make anew the same universe? Had you been here you would have said, "There is no one here," whether you expected to find God or had set out to prove there was no God. But that you said is the original name of God when encountered for the first time by anyone not there that was not invited by him to come, "No One Here." Who then did you expect to find, one like you? Are you God? Are you the Most High God by himself? God is invisible. No one can see God even God. When he looks at himself he sees no one there for that is all of No One There anyone, not Elohim, not Yahweh, not Joshua, not Mizraim or me or anyone not a God in God with God in them for none of them are holy from the origin which is No One There, God and he has no name for no one even there is permitted to utter any name that indicates anything there for it is the original holy place the most holy place that can be thought by anyone. Only Elohim, Yahweh, Joshua and some of those that have been made Gods in God have been there and have become No One There while they were there. They could be seen the moment they were created but not one of them has ever seen No One There as he originally was, is and will always be without end.

That is whom he is and there is not, never was and never will be anyone more holy for even to call him No One There defiles his person for he is there. Can anyone prove differently? Is he not No One There for where he was in that time where there was no time he is as no one to all that come to that time and that place. He is all that is real. All else is an illusion compared to him and all those illusion that think they think in their own mind finding him to be an illusion when they are the illusion and in themselves can only know other illusions and nothing of reality, all that is real, him and all the true illusions that were made. He made space. He made it empty. He made it endless distance.

He did not make time. A man saw differently than God did and the illusion of linear time began. Now he has made all things not in no time but in time, linear time that we may understand. The reason he cannot be seen is space is an illusion and he was before time and in no time at all he created everything that was created, all things that can be created. When he saw the illusion of time that the man made. It was the man thinking in his mind and he knew it too was a true illusion even before the man did.

So it was not that anyone created anything new. The man saw it and God saw it for what a man thinks he also thinks when a man is in him, has become insane or has become evil and not in him. All of thought is God's thoughts and all that is thought, everything that was thought or ever will be thought is God's thoughts though some he has intentionally forgotten and hopes never to think again.

Nearly every thought that can be thought has been thought with an infinite number of times and even now proceeds to be thought again and again toward an infinite number of infinite numbers of times. There are then a limited number of thoughts and God has thought them all and knows any meaning they might have. He is all knowing and omniscient not just partially that.

Think about what you are thinking then. Did you intend to think that? Was it one of the random things God created? Is it a new thought to you? Would you if you were God want yourself thinking such a thing when all that you think is in his mind?

The insane think things they cannot handle. Some think things that torment them and would torment God if he allowed them to.

Do not think such things. There is an infinite number of things to think. Think something else if you are not mentally ill and therefore have no power over what you may think without your thinker was corrupted before you were born so that your thoughts have all been beyond your ability to choose the one from the other.

The evil think things God will not think, never did and never will but they have thought them all seeming to be in him when all they are is in his thoughts and are not, never were and never will be in him if they keep thinking things God wills not to think though he knows them the same as he knows everything.

God knows all evil. He had not thought any evil when he was to be known as No One There, not the one that is seen in that form but the one he really is for to see God and even think, "There is no one there," is to blaspheme God for he is there and everyone to see there and think that is evil to that extent.

All evil comes from misunderstanding and all misunderstanding was born the first time God was seen and someone understood there was no one there. Thus even his name is an affront to who he is and the words used to say what it appears to be, he is or is not is a lie and a flagrant sin. The Most High God, the Only God and the God with no name are the only proper names for God anything else is sinful and an evil illusion of what he should be called No One There though we have no other way to say that in English than those very words. God forgive me. I am English. I speak English and that is the same in any other language and demeans your holy person to say who you were in the beginning before you made anything in the place where there was no time which does not come ever again for all is created in linear time here.

It took God three minutes to create the universe the exact universe the old one was he sped time up so much so that all of time could be in linear time with the creation of the old universe being first made in no time at all experienced in the amount of time it was experience but finished in no time with this universe that far ahead in time, three exact minutes doing everything ever done and making anything ever made exactly as it had been done in the old universe for there is no limitation on what the Most High God can do anymore than there was for, God forgive me for using that sinful name to indicate you again, No One There.

We are in time but we can move through time in the time it takes for us to notice we are there. If only you would believe and ask to see Yahweh's face, the face of the Most High God and be changed. But no one alive on the New Earth has seen God's face though some have requested to. It takes faith to see God's face and faith they do not have. Very few can even hear him or believe they feel his present with most not even noticing any difference when he is present or when he is not though God is always present and he simply gives us that illusion for we understand only illusions that he is there.

The Most High God is there even when we do not know it and when we fall away and turn evil. There is no place truly that God is not whether in space or time or even in our thoughts. We simply do not pay attention to him past the point we can consciously realize he is there. In some even their subliminal thoughts that he is there are ignored past the point they have any effect on us in some cases. But beware. He is there and he can do anything to us or for us even should we not believe in any way.

The only thing truly beyond God is the perfect darkness he believes he can feel and that we can feel and he has never believed anything that was false for it is impossible for him to do that though some believe he was only feeling what he is and what is in his Being. Even then it is best to believe the way God does just as with that name No One There, God forgive me again, for it leads you to a misunderstanding and is potentially evil for it is actually moot for in truth it is a thing that is felt by all of your feelings and nothing else like an empty space in the shadow of a planet where there is not light to a blind any of man though in such a place all that are not God would be blind, but I say that simply to give an idea what it is like for God. Staring out at the darkness sooner or later turns the mind inward toward being within it.

We are actually a spirit as God is a Spirit, an orb outside of God that glows according to the amount we do as God does and believe as God does. Our illusions actually are not illusions but what God intuited had to be outside him, the very thing we think we are in our minds in that very environment and we are sensing what he intuited all along was there for us to experience and we all do. All that goes on in our minds goes on in his mind and what goes on in our minds is what we sense of what actually is. We can have different opinions about what actually is, than God. It is a matter of how bright we shine in that in the pure darkness beyond God.

Yahweh's glare was brighter than anyone else. He is more there than the rest of us are is why. What is true out here is our interactions not our thinking and what proper thinking is to be here is to think like Yahweh though Most High God knows everything we think and there are no more things to think so he knows it all just the same anyway.

When one is destroyed their light goes out. When they are brought back their light returns to them. The evil are like a bubble in the darkness like blowing bubbles at midnight visible only because of the light of the good.

Yahweh is very nearly perfect goodness and God Most High is only as bright as Yahweh, Jesus' Father, the Father of the saints and Gods saved by Christ. We are all just hanging around out here interacting with our minds and our spirits. Our spirits are not actually in us but another of us that is part of our team.

Those with psychological demons in us have dark spots in us. The mentally ill and all the insane are a terrible mess of bright light and dark spots constantly moving but going no where almost randomly, an internal randomness made by someone other than Most High God and they move around willy-nilly. They are all over the place. The evil are doing the same thing and some of them have bright spots in them.

The Devil and the anti-Chist, Beal are all bright but the saved devils and demons have bright spots in them and stay in one place. The brightness of any one of our spheres is determined by the number of dark spots in them. It is an entirely different way of knowing God never thought of before, the sort of thing I seem to be always doing.

There is no telling the things God may come to know. There is no difference in color they are all just bright white light. Those that do not believe in God either have no orb or they cannot be seen. They do not believe and are not anything.

But the Buddhists have some that are very bright, not like God but bright. So it appears it is not all a belief in God but how good one is that helps them really be here. Very few on the New Earth have spheres and this may be a means of identifying who they are we can reach. God is leaving them that want to be there out there and returning to his own thoughts.

They all know him there. That alone is worth the knowing. Out there one is really what one is in reality. Even those of different times are all in the same place in that outer darkness where when it began God saw nothing and thought he was actually feeling it which he was with all his feeling ability. That's the same as it is on earth where nothing can actually be touched. There is always some small amount of space between things.

Now some of these orbs have come to be when God was all involved in his own thinking. They are complete strangers to God. He has no idea what they are thinking. But they are communicating. The Most High God asked them after sharing his mind with them if there was anything else to learn and they replied there was not.

God is satisfied that is true. He knows the secrets to all being just as they do apparently. They were unaware in a sense as to what God was doing for they did not care, but they are intrigued by being seen though most of them do not care.

God can move around but they all notice him when he does. It appears to be unacceptable behavior to move. He moved out beyond them and there never seems to be any end to them and there is room for an infinite number right here. Heaven is gigantic!!!

By taking my suggestion and taking himself out into his environment God discovered all of reality not just what was in his mind since the time he found what appeared to be no one or anything he could see.

That is the way they all were before they began to be good and shine in the darkness that went on seemingly without end when God gave up looking for an end to it. But it was full of an infinite number of Gods all spheres of light shining with all goodness and a much smaller number of evil ones that were completely dark orbs that were distinguishable only by the light from the good ones. He added all of us, Gods and mankind to that number and them already out there were amazed at what he is doing in his mind and plans to continue doing without requiring they be good only in his way.

God took us all in and combined our light with his light and the light of all mankind. Now we are by far the brightest one God saw out there all of us put together. They require now only that you be good here in heaven, for lack of a better word, and he will share his goodness with absolutely anyone here that even the most vile and evil among us may add to our light; to our goodness. All goodness here in the New Heaven and the New Earth is a part of all goodness and will be shared with all of those out there beyond God in reality, a reality he has intuitively created in his mind and will continue to make the Gods that are out there in his mind too.

This is as much Heaven for God the same as it is Heaven for all even mankind on earth even some aliens who were all thought to be ignorant and of no real concern will be joined with our light if they desire and in fact some have when they found out what was going on while God was all wrapped up in his thoughts figuring out what and who had to be out there as it appears they all like God began to follow his lead. It is an entire new deal and we can talk to them out there if they will talk to us the same as we can talk to God.

The long range goal I ask God Most High right now is to help everyone in reality to overcome being evil and even those evil ones in the minds of the orbs of light to overcome being evil that will cooperate or even hopefully in time ask, right?

"Definitely," Most High God replied.

Just think there are probably others out there that think like I do, an anomaly that Yahweh made that did not think like God and maybe an infinite number of us at least. God took on the light from one of those he met out there and has returned thinking like I do and with our collective goodness in him in his mind is the brightest orb God saw in the entire area of reality we are in what appears to go on without end in all directions, an endless sky filled with what looks like an infinite number of stars far away to bright shiny spheres the closer one is to the rest of us.

A good spirit is bright and gives off light limited only by the amount of light it gives off and its goodness. One day no one in all of reality ever need not be good for the evil ones are avoided and ignored out here until they become frustrated and destroy themselves and that they were goes back to the original form they were in just like all the Gods that have all always been here and only started being good long about the time our God the First Good God first appeared in this area at least and perhaps the first in all of reality. That's the Most High God. Reality has always been conscious but was neither good or evil not concerned about either until Most High God, No One There began to glow and lit up like the first star ever to be in any sky.

So this is what I saw when in fiction they suggested there was that well beyond God in the time he is in now; the truth. It was all light everywhere so it looked to me, but it must have been this.

WOW!!! WAKE UP AND LET YOUR LIGHT SHINE!!.

5 WHAT REALITY ACTUALLY IS AND LOOKS LIKE

In essence he was a tiny sphere of darkness in darkness. No one not even God could tell him from that empty place that was there when God created him. He was the least thing God could think of as being. He was so tiny and indistinguishable from the rest of that often called nothing that is supposedly comprised of nothingness.

But he was there. He had to be knowable for he is now though no one but God has ever seen him in his mind that was not using his mind to know he was there for he was indistinguishable from the rest of unconscious darkness with no virtue, meaning no goodness of any kind at all. He was known, he was a tiny sphere and he was darkness, that is all; like a neutrino except he was conscious on the high side and unconscious on the low side and what comprised him was spirit, that between completely unconscious and conscious existence. He existed for there is not anything that does not exist that can be known except that which is yet to be created.

If nothing exists and I doubt that it does it is not comprised of tiny spheres like him. It cannot be known even intuitively. And it is not even dark and comprised by darkness. But there is no such thing but an illusion in the mind of the thinker that is not true. It is not even fiction.

Therefore he was fiction on the lesser side. He was really a spirit in essence. But on the high side he was intuitively known by God and no one else for God knew, knows and will know every thing and every one. He is the same as you are whether you are in the mind of God or outside of God and therefore real just as God is real, a spirit and essentially everything that he was.

She was the same when later she came to be.

He was created six days after the beginning of all unconscious things that were created by the God with no name. He that created him was I Am That I Am, the I am, Almighty God, Yahweh, the Father of Christ, God. He was created by El Eloi in the Being of Elohim, the Thee, the Trinity, God and he was essentially the same one as he was. El Eloi was created by random things which were created by the God with no name who had always been conscious, memorable to God because he has seen him and known him all the time he has existed and he was essentially the same as he was.

But the God with no name was destined to create reality in his mind. Now we do not need to only be in the mind of God the way it was before who is the Only God who is the Most High God but now also the God of Reality for he has incorporated all of Reality in him we can now also see.

They are essentially the same. He has much virtue though some of his virtue is wasted not likened to the God of Reality whose knowledge is greater than any one's, he knew everything, knows everything and will know everything and that is true for any one also. His virtue is unsurpassed in the Reality that is in the God of Reality and when his sphere broke it joined the virtue of all Reality as did the God of Reality's virtue. Now it is theirs. They are both in that which surrounds every reality.

The one that does his thinking and experiencing is God's me, the one that does God's thinking and experiencing. He is God.

He was called the man. He was called Adam. He was named John Fredrick Carver. He was nicknamed Jack and Jackie. He took back his original name John. He is yet John to his friends to this moment, the moment in which he is only a man, sitting at his laptop keyboarding this in his apartment in his hometown in

Minnesota, in the United States of America on the Northern continent of the Western Hemisphere on the planet earth in the solar system where he was created in the Milky Way in the spiral system the Milky way is in and in the universe God created in three minutes in the combination of two identical universes the one being created in six days but in the second dimension in the mind of God as it was before he took all of Reality into him but his virtue is limitless.

He saw the great light. Now he is in the great light. But he is everywhere in all knowable time and space. Anything beyond him is a waste of virtue for what purpose would such virtue be if it is not even knowable by him or anyone else. To attribute any more virtue to him is to waste virtue. He like his creator is what he is. He is that he is. The God with this great virtue is not a God yet. He is but an old man with a great future.

You also are as he was. He was the man. He was Adam who is alive and well at the moment outside the mind of God the way it was where he likes to be but we of Adam from Eve to the last one born in God's mind then or made outside the mind of God then are Adam, the man, he unless you are Yahweh, Almighty God, the Father of Christ; Joshua, Jesus Christ, the Son of God, Mizraim the Spirit of God, the Holy Ghost, the Holy Spirit of Elohim, the Three, the Trinity, God, the God with no name, an angel or angelic spirit you are Adam like me and your me is the God with no name's me even as are all mes that were given to anyone ever created in the mind of God.

Every one ever to be in the mind of God as it was before is God but one who exists in God's mind that was taken from the Reality outside the reality that was only in the mind of God, the God with no name in either dimension whether the one Satan is in at present or the one he is not in at present, the one wherein heaven has come meaning both dimensions and earth and the part with those left behind or those on earth in the mind of God or outside the mind of God in his Reality, a Reality that is now in him now the God of Reality.

Everything in the mind of God before all reality was taken in by him is true. Everything outside the mind of God at that time is

Real as were all things in the mind of God then . This is Reality and my words are true. Good is good and any part of that goodness, all virtue is good except that virtue that is not knowable which is a waste.

Judge any wickedness and evil that exists for evil is encased in a thick and hardening darkness that it may not contaminate our goodness but even evil when it is beneficial is goodness and everyone will be forgiven even if they are evil in me and in the God with no name. He knows all evil and its ways the same as he knows all of goodness though he remains very good. We, him and me are a team.

In the name of my rightful Father, Yahweh, I proclaim these words that my rightful holy Brother, Jesus may have a starting point to judge the truth as I see it, to find me lacking or to support it. I am neither my Father, my rightful Father nor my Brother but all that I know is in the mind of God, the God with no name, the one you may access in the Holy Spirit, the Spirit of God also known as Mizraim in love. I am in Elohim also then.

We love you. I and my Father forever. There is nothing you can do to make us not love you except completely destroy us which is possible. All of those who are Adam and all others even the alien among us; welcome. My Father supports me in this truth. That we do as a team is higher than that we do selfishly. That is of our own doing, saying and even thinking.

Therefore make the mind of God your own mind if you are of a mind to do that, have full knowledge and be wise and loving. To not forgive anything including any evil is not wise for it is unloving and limits ones virtue. Strive then to have the greatest virtue possible for you to have. May your virtue be greater than mine if it is not wasted with regard to yourself and others both in the same instance. There are many different kinds of virtue some limiting and some not limiting in any way. But there is only one goodness.

There was then for us one reality, the reality that was in the Most High God's mind. That doubled and became two dimensions, to identical universes when heaven that was not received came to earth. Then the Most High God took us out of his mind and into

Reality and we could pass back and forth between the reality that was in his mind and the Reality that is real the same as it was real in God's mind. We still see each other and the universe as we did before when Really we are spheres floating around earth with the aliens floating around the rest of our universe. But we, those on earth and those in our two heavenly places are all Real in Reality, that which is the same as that which was in Most High God's mind at one time. It is fine to see them either way. Mankind seems to prefer seeing themselves as men and women moving around on earth. The aliens seem to have taken to being in outer space where they see themselves as orbs as they always did. Our way is a common illusion that limits our interaction with the rest of those in heaven which is now a place where they manifest any way they want to some orbs but most not though to a visitor we all appear to be what we are orbs of light or orbs clothed by thick and even hardened dark surfaces. All of those views on perceptions are valid in anyone's mind that was in the old earth or in the old heaven.

May goodness and love and any true virtue I might have be with you as is the God with no name with you in all his ways. Amen..

6 AWKWARD BEGINNING

When me and the God with no name took our virtue or light and him his mind out as far as we could when I began to save those I should love the least we came to a place I had seen in a vision I called the great light for at the time I was spirited away by Beal and saw nothing in the mind of the God with no name but I went beyond him into that which was his surroundings in search of the original God which is I believe the God with no name, the same one who is now the God of Reality whom I would like to say did it on purpose but it is just his way.

He always is on the beam to being the original one to pursue truth which most of those in reality do not even understand let alone comprehend. So he has done it again. Having intuitively created the real universe as we would call it he found that he was well equipped now he learned love from me to be larger than all of his environment very nearly and had far out shined any one in his reality with his enormous knowledge knowing every thing that could be thought by one within his own mind.

As it turns out there are an infinite number of infinite areas around each God in it and an infinite number of Gods usually one to each one though one has four Gods in his reality that she made. He intuitively knew it was fine for us to burst our sphere and spread our consciousnesses out beyond all of them after taking every God in his reality into his mind without once blowing his mind as I prophesied he would not if he did it more gradually than all at once.

Now he is confronted with a new Reality wherein those who have encompassed their own reality are all good to the full extent of their spheres. He encompasses his entire reality and knows everything good and evil in that entire reality and interacts with those who did not dare burst their sphere for the ones to do it before blew their minds.

It is pure virtue out there in the light, the great light. Once again we are effectively in his mind again with only one difference. He did not create it. He was merely the first to be God and to intuit what his surroundings would be well enough to easily adapt to being the first God to not only become the God of his reality but to in effect be the God of that Reality wherein the Gods of their own reality are in his knowledge and he in pure virtue. And, I had the privilege of being there and experiencing what we did in the same procedure.

He is therefore the God of All Realities and it is pure knowledge and pure virtue. When I saw it my mind was nearly blown just by the sight of it and now I am part of it too having the mind of the Most High God to access any part of it and him sharing all my virtue which began to really grow when I forgave Satan, Beal and the rest of the underworld what all they had ever done to me which was incredibly horrible and saved them who are now good though once they were evil.

Here in heaven on earth where it has finally come down to though it always was actually here I an old man looking out now to the great light where the invisible God is invisible once more joined by Elohim and those in him, Yahweh, Jesus Christ and Mizraim in the mind of the God of All Reality where there is an area that is an infinite distance in its radius and dark with no Gods here, an infinite void. In the infinite void there are two spheres with three smaller spheres in one of them.

Instantly Elohim works a miracle and a huge blue planet appears as the two major orbs mine many times the other, Yahweh, and in Yahweh's orb three tiny spheres, Elohim, Joshua and

Mizraim. The two of us Yahweh and me orbit the planet with the three smaller ones forming a triangle in Yahweh and circle the planet to give it light and warmth throughout the entire daytime and the nighttime, me the daylight and Yahweh the nighttime light, a full day averaging 23 hours.

From the surface it looks like two suns in the sky and a seemingly endless number of stars that are so bright they travel an infinite distance hidden by that distance between us and them. There are no stars in its sky just us five orbs.

All spirits are orbs and we being spirits are then merely orbs of light giving off heat enough also to keep the planet warm both day and night. On the planet there are one hundred people scattered throughout its surface in fifty pairs spread far enough apart they are not likely to interact for some time if they are human which they appear to be. But closer observation reveals that they are not actually human. They do not have sex organs.

Sex when it occurred on earth after the fiasco with Satan in Paradise turned out to have been a mistake. The inhabitants of Eden went sex crazy and the punishment turned out to be in their eyes a phenomenal reward that took over a very large part of their attention if you remember the first earth, the one created in just six days from virtually a mind virtually empty of living higher life forms except for the dolphins being the only other notable intelligence on that planet created in its only creation that resulted in every human being, made there becoming evil and destroying itself by the God with no name, the Spirit of God and El Eloi before he created Elohim and the others that were in him at the time of the second creation of mankind that lived in Eden, Paradise at first.

They were each walking along the shore of various bodies of water in silence before God volunteered to go to them to break the ice.

"What do I say?" he asked the others. "Let me think."

They appeared to be about eighteen, have dark hair and are of a grayish sort of black complexion with dark eyes and bright shiny teeth. The weather is such that they are all naked. We had expected they would be saying something. But they did not.

"Did you speak?" he said to them all at the same time.

There was no reply.

"Just say, 'Hi,'" I suggested.

Silence.

"Where are we?" one of them, a female asked.

"You are on Planet," I said.

"We know that," she said, thinking I had said, "'A Planet.'"

"As far as you can see or go in any direction is called Planet," I replied after giving it some thought.

"We're on a planet called Planet?" she asked.

"Do you have another name for it," I replied, "It is your planet. We give it to you."

"Who are we?" she asked.

"I call you, Man and Woman," I said.

"Why?" she asked.

"Because he is a man and you are a woman," I replied. "Would you prefer I called you something else?"

"My yes," she said.

"I call you Shuvah," I said, "And you I call Adam."

Silence.

"Do you like your names?" I asked them.

They looked at each other but said nothing.

"Shuvah," I said, "Meet Adam."

They looked at each other curiously and frowned to think I had introduced them to each other.

"If you do not want those names pick one for the other one," I said.

"Why?" she said.

"So that you will be able to call the other one something more than you or just start talking to them," I said, "Don't you think that is a good idea?"

They obviously didn't know what to say.

"A name is a gift one gives to another to identify them as not themselves and then hopes they will repay the kindness by giving them a name also," I said.

"Shy," he said.

"Do you mean to call her by that name?" I asked somewhat surprised.

"I am shy," he said.

"That's okay," I said. "It is natural to be a little awkward at first."

"That is what this is," she said, "Awkward. How did you know?"

"You are a man and a woman," I said, "My name is John. I am God."

"What is that you have on your body?" one of them asked.

"Clothing," I said yet surprised they knew what things were called. "How do you know what things are called?" I asked in curiosity.

"Can I have some?" she asked and I thought I understood that they were awkward because they were naked.

"Are you sure you want some?" I asked.

She frowned.

"They are far more uncomfortable than the way you are not dressed," I said.

She felt of the sleeve of my shirt.

He did not. He put his hand on his bare chest where there was hair.

"You look like us in every way," she said. "Are you sure you are not a man?"

"Yes," I said, "We have some very basic differences. I would like to have you meet a friend of mine. Would that be okay?"

She put her head down slightly but continued to look at me and I realized she must frown when she is puzzled but took it to mean it would be okay.

"He is a God also," I said, "When you see him you will be changed and know all the things you want to know that the Most High knows."

Then I hesitated and asked Yahweh to show himself in my mind. He showed his face.

"Tell me," I said, "What do you see?"

"A man," she said.

"He just looks like a man the same as I do," I said. "He is another of God."

"My he's big!" she said.

I said nothing.

She looked up into his face.

"What did you notice?" I asked her, "Anything?"

"I see that I am God," she said without frowning.

"Now you are God the same as I am God and he is God," I said and she nodded. "Would you like to look at him and be the same?" I urged Adam, but he looked at the ground.

"What are you writing?" she said. I was surprised she knew what writing was. But I was writing this in my man at my home on earth to show you how it actually went. Then instantly understanding she frowned and asked, "Why are you doing that?" I was amazed that she really wanted to know so it seemed. Then realizing again she was perplexed. "This is very strange to me," she said and I wondered for a moment, 'Why was I doing it really?' Then I realized it was what I do when I am involved in anything God does; write about it and this new creation seemed fascinating to me.

He looked at her noticing that she had not changed but there was something different about her. Then he looked up into Yahweh's face. Then he looked away very abruptly.

"What did you understand?" I asked him.

"I am God," he mumbled. "My name is the name of the first man."

"Adam?" I asked.

"He died," he managed.

"He is alive now," I said, "In a place very far away. Would you like to speak to him?"

He put his head to the side and down very quickly.

"It is okay not to want to talk to him," I said before I asked him, "But why not? Your name?"

"It is the same," he said.

"That is good," I said, "You have the something in common."

He put his head even farther back to the right and tried not to peer at me.

"You don't have to," I said, "You are free to do what you would like."

He looked at the female and seemed to stare with wide eyes.

I took it as my cue to leave. I am not sure why. So I just turned and walked away to where the lake shore bent to the right away from the lake, stepped back up into the grass away from the beach and vanished to return to the sky though my orb was there all this time. I had merely manifested as a man. Then I went back into my sphere and reunited with myself.

They looked at each other and sighed.

Then after a short time they continued to walk the beach in the way I had gone in the same manner they had been walking before my first conversation with them, me deciding it had not gone too well.

"Leave that to me," Yahweh said.

"How did you know it was me?" Yahweh said later.

"I recognized your voice," I said, "Elohim rarely uses your voice. That or he does and I don't realize it isn't you.

After a while Elohim said, "Fascinating."

"Let's try another one," Elohim suggested later.

"Who's first?" he asked a short time after.

"It didn't go well," Elohim said, "Maybe we should try something else?"

Someone thought maybe Yahweh should give them a command like he did Adam in Paradise. It was Most High.

"Man," Yahweh said. Then he added, "What should I tell him?" Then after giving it some thought he said, "You know who I am. I am God. Walk out into the water."

The man heard the voice he used but looked spooked and looked around. Then he looked up. Then down at the water. After that he did not hesitate. He walked out in the water up to his chin.

"Stop!" Yahweh said.

He stopped.

"Now turn around and go back to shore," Yahweh said.

He did.

"You have heard my voice," Yahweh said, "And you have obeyed me. That is good. It shall go well with thee."

"This is starting to get boring," I commented.

"That is enough for today," Yahweh said.

Someone later asked, "What is wrong with them?"

"Maybe we should give them something to eat," I suggested.

"They don't eat. We supply all their needs," they said.

7 LEARNING THROUGH PAIN

I played a game with one of them.

I said, "Can you count?"

He didn't know what I meant so I took him through counting to two in his language, English and he got the idea right away. He saw what I was saying.

"If you take the distance between your to hands and take one hand away how much distance is there?"

He said, "There isn't any."

"Sure there is," I said. "How far can you go before you reach your other hand that way?"

"Beyond all things," he said.

"What is beyond all of them?" I asked.

"More things," he said.

"And, what is beyond those things?" I asked.

"More things again," he said.

Then I asked, "What if you come to a place where counting any more things is tedious and boring to the point you just can't bring yourself to count one more thing? What is beyond that?"

"I don't know," he said.

"Could you ever know?" I asked.

"Not if I don't start up again," he said.

"But you have counted all you can bear to count. How can you bare to count anymore than that even if you rest along the way?"

"I can't," he said.

"Do you know what that is called?" I asked.

"No," he said.

"Well, if you are God and know everything you would reach a point where their was no reason to count any more and no purpose in counting any more."

"What's that called?" he asked.

"Infinity," I said.

"Infinity?" he said, "So that's what that is."

"But you know there is more than that. How many infinities are there?" I asked.

"I could start all over and count them all," he said.

"But you might come to the same problem for you would count all the numbers by giving them all the names there are for anything and then you could name them all the words in your language then the names of all the sounds you could make or think, then name all the thoughts you could think until in the end you would be seeing more but you got confused as to how many for you had run out of things to call them. That is infinity too," I said.

He was amazed.

"Then you could start all over by counting all the infinities that made up, but there wouldn't be much point in what you were doing because you don't really know how many you have counted. It's just a number that has no meaning to you. Do you know what that's called?" I asked. "That's impractical infinity. You count them until they have no meaning or purpose to them and those beyond that are impractical right after the last one that had any purpose or meaning or that was practical. So that is practical infinity. How many are there in impractical infinity?"

"My head hurts. My brain hurts!" he said.

"That's alright just let it go on up through the top of your head and forget about it. It will slowly stop hurting. Then don't picture it anymore. Just realize there is a difference between impractical infinity and practical infinity and don't try to picture it anymore," I said.

"I did that," he said, "It just keeps hurting."

"It will stop," I said, "Just relax your brain and think about something else."

"Kangaroos?" he said.

"Do you like kangaroos? Why?" I asked.

"I like the way they look and the sound of their name, kangaroo. Kangaroo!" he said.

"Do you like to box?" I said.

"What is that?" he asked.

"Just walk up to one and try to hit it," I said.

So he did.

"It blocks my every try!" he said, having fun.

Then it began to attempt to hit him and it finally did.

"That hurts!" he said and backed away. "But it was sure fun!"

"You see," I said, "There is good pain and there is bad pain. Kangaroos are some of the best boxers there are. But having your mind blown always hurts and it can make you so confused you don't make sense until God changes you back to the way you were except you know better than to do it again."

'What did you try to hit me for?' the kangaroo asked him with its thoughts.

"He told me to," he said. "Did you mind?"

'I didn't like it at first but then it was fun,' the kangaroo said and hopped away.

"If you want to get good at boxing keep trying to hit her," I said. "Then when you hit her she will stop and just hop away. But don't hit her again. That would be mean."

"I don't want to be mean," he said.

"And don't ever hurt the woman here with you," I said, "It will scare her."

"Why?" he asked.

"She already knows you are bigger and stronger than she is and she trusts you not to hurt her and she will be afraid of you after that," I said.

"It was fun, boxing with that kangaroo!" he said. "But it hurt!!"

Then I began to write down our conversation according to my memory of it when he asked, "What would happen if I hit you?"

"I wouldn't like it," I replied.

"What would you do?" I said.

"It would hurt and I would hurt you back," I replied, "I can hurt your head without touching you. What do you think I could do to you by touching you?"

"Nothing," he said.

"Yeah, right," I said.

He laughed.

"Is your head better?" I asked him.

"A little better but it still hurts," he said, "Especially if I think about it hurting."

"Do your best not to think about it then," I said, "And rest. You can even go to sleep. It will be better yet when you wake up. I am sorry about that. I didn't realize what it was doing to you until it was too late. You were picturing all that, weren't you? Forgive me?"

"Are you sure I will be alright?" he asked.

I prophesied he would be and then dared to tell him he would.

He didn't say anything but he forgave me for finally he said, "I forgave you."

"Will I be okay?" he asked later.

"Yes you will," I said, "Just don't think about it. When you start to think about it, distract yourself with something else like the woman here with you."

"She is really neat," he said excitedly, "Thank you."

"Thank Almighty God," I said, "He made her and you just the way you are."

"Thanks Almighty God," he said.

Then he started talking to Yahweh.

The truth is like that. It can hurt your brain if you think about it too hard. It can be cruel like a splitting headache from picturing something to understand it and concentrating too hard. It can result in unwanted consequences like when the kangaroo hit him. Even that can be fun if no one gets angry or hurt to badly.

But to beat them which means to hit them again when they have had enough and try to get away, that would be true but it would be mean and it is not good to be mean. The moment I realized I had hurt his brain by simply talking to him I stopped. But he was hurt and is still hurting and will be for some time. He may always remember the experience, the first time he had his mind blown. Much can be learned that way but it is painful and potentially it can leave one so confused they don't ever make sense again or in other words go insane so that only Most High can cure them.

To do what I did to him on purpose is not good and may even be evil. But not to stop the moment you realize you are causing someone pain is brutal and should never be done. But if this happens to you forgive it anyway whether they meant to do it or not. If you do you have beaten their effort to intimidate even your thoughts about it for a long time and when you remember it, it won't have any effect on you for it is in the past and you survived.

There was no evil here. What I did was not evil? I was ignorant to his pain. It was a mistake so I had to turn it into a good mistake. He learned the difference between fun and good pain and bad pain. But more importantly he learned how to forgive and to thank God for the good things he has done even to just giving him his woman and as I suggested his life.

"You're great," someone said to which I reply a simple, "Thank you."

"I love you, John," they said and it makes it all worth while. I pray you do also. Amen.

Thinking is real activity with tangible results and consequences.

Note: I have been taken to task by Elohim and Jesus. It is not for what I did in making a mistake concerning the man only to immediately cease what I was doing and make it right. That is not only good it is part of the New Way. It is publishing this on earth which will hurt many people's brains on purpose and potentially blow some humans' minds and they will have to be fixed by Most High though they will be changed which is good.

But it is not part of the New Way and is an error against being loving and the New Way is to be loving and good. I was good by sharing this and though you doubtlessly learned from it those who learned anything from it it was not a loving act to hurt your brain. I apologize and beg you to forgive me and then love me for this I do now also.

To those that do I am yet in the new way for Most High has judged the New Way as evil, Yahweh has forgiven me for he has passed on judging this good or evil. Of course Mizraim has also judged me to be good and that is all that matters to her. Only Jesus and Elohim have a bone to pick with me about it not being allowed in the New Way. But now that I do this even Elohim and Jesus forgive me. Thus I may remain in the New Way and I am yet good..

8 THE OVERVIEW OF THE MOST HIGH GOD

The smallest possible place is not a place that God has seen yet but it does exist. It is a place so tiny that God has gone down into his mind in search of the idea and the search is without end. The smallest practical place is a sphere so tiny that God can only intuit that it is there. There are an infinite number of them in the tiniest elemental particle's area.

When he became practical that is what he was and in fact he was the first one of those ever. But he was it so briefly that any shorter length of time is impractical. There is an infinite number of them in an hour. With twenty four times that number in a day on out to an infinite number of hours that have passed so far with unceasing multiples of that long in unending time and so much longer it is totally impractical to measure linear time in any knowable amount of time.

Everything in any distance and time existed in the same tiny length of time and appears also to have no ending. All things are not actually knowable in essence or to their full extent of time and space. It is entirely possible that an infinite number of minds using concepts other than space and time exist coincidentally without our understanding of the essence of thought and the full extent of what may be thought.

The Most High God already knows them all. They are all in

him. None of them know we exist or have ever interacted with us even to pay us attention. God has paid attention to them all and knows all about them. They are relatively tiny compared to our sphere of existence and were short lived and the consciousnesses in them are always the same one.

Most High God never created what once was his environment but now is incorporating it in his mind. He yet has an environment that he has concluded has no end. It was all created at once in the same moment and it has all always been and it all might have occurred in that very same moment, a moment that will be repeated until it fills all of time eventually for there is an end to time. God Most High has been to the end of time many times and can go to any place in it and it seems a very short distance.

He is taking his time incorporating it all because he does not want to blow his mind. He already knows he incorporated it all in his mind. So long as he continues to love and be loved he will not have an end. But worshiping him impairs his virtue but not his mind.

He began evil and will be evil in the end. I will be there loving him anyway and forgiving any evil he ever did. He will go on to create evil to as great of an extent as is possible but my virtue as it stands out there right now will destroy it and convert him in the end of it when he knows not only all goodness as he knew here in this time but every possible evil in the next.

Then he will be good again for endless time unless something happens to change his mind namely Satan who may destroy him out of pity for him and die himself. But in that case his legacy of knowledge will not be left behind until he comes again and starts all over again to do it all again but better that time and each time thereafter until there is no reason to do it again or no purpose served by him doing it even one more time so it will all turn out to have been practical all that time and even then he will not die without end.

He has given the New Way authority to change it all as we come up behind him again and again..

9 WHAT IS SPIRIT

"Do you know what you are?" I asked my friend that I blew his mind.

He looked at his body thinking I was talking about gender.

"You are spirit," I said.

His eyes opened wide with interest but he said nothing. I suspected because he did not know what I was talking about.

"A spirit," I said, "Is—well?" I spread my arms out in such a way as to indicate the entire area. Then I said, "The entire place of all distance like we talked about that hurt your head is called space." Then I took a place before both our heads for we were standing and after that I said, "This is space. Now if we put something in that space what do we have?"

"What we put into it?" he said.

"What happened to the space that was there then?" I asked.

"It went away," he said.

"Let's see," I said and stilling the breeze I made a soap bubble appear out of the spirit and float in the space I had indicated.

He was delighted.

"Now, we had the space but now we have a bubble in the space and you say the space went away. But did it?" I said and took the bubble out of the place back into the spirit making it

50

disappear and destroying it. "Let's see," I said, "The space did not go anywhere. It is yet there. Is it not?"

He looked at it in puzzlement. "There were two things there?" he said.

I nodded.

"Space and that pretty thing?" he said.

"That is almost right," I said. "But they would have been all smooshed together if not for the most important part. The spirit is there keeping them apart."

He felt of his head again and I began to wonder if he was picturing it and since he could not it was beginning to hurt his brain again.

I did not want to do that again so I expounded hoping to leave it at that since he might be able to figure out what I was talking about anyway. "That is what we are. Where you are there once was just an empty space. Then they made you and put you in the first place you ever were. You are a spirit not empty space. You are a spirit not a body. You keep empty space and your body from getting all smooshed together," I explained.

"Me?" he said too amazed to be confused at my explanation that was really explained the way Most High God had explained it to me done differently.

But he experienced everything after it happens; not long, just a moment or two later. When you are in the spirit you are actually doing everything you are doing and everything that happens in you or around you happens. In what happens next it is the same way. There is a present, where everything is spirit happening in spirit, God, the present. With that pain yesterday in what has already happened all he had to do was say, "Stop!" in the present, in the Spirit of God, the present, remember? It would have stopped. He would have felt no more pain and no pain any longer as time went along either."

His eyes were very wide open and sparkled in the light from my sphere above.

"You can have anything you want, too," I said. "Just say in the present, God's Spirit, what you want and it will be in the present that same moment and you being a little tiny bit in the past remembering what you experienced will experience it in the normal way you always do a moment or two in the past in your memory and not as you really experienced it firsthand if you hold onto it and let be that long."

Before I had finished speaking he made a live fish appear right in his hand by just thinking of one in the present. We are too often a moment in that which has passed remembering the present, what we actually experienced. No one can actually go to the past. But we can do things to it in God's Spirit.

We can forget it and it is nowhere in us. It may still be in other people's memory but it is not in ours. We can add something to it that changes how hurtful it was. We can forgive them for doing it and forget they did it. Then it is almost gone. All that is left to do is forget what it was. We will never forget it and it will be in our memory forever if we never just try to forget it."

There are a number of ways to forget things. We can do as God does and simply say it is not, not anything and forget it ever was anything because then it is not anything, was not anything in the beginning and that same thing cannot be anything in the future because we can do anything we want to to empty space and what is in empty space or that took place in empty space even to destroy it simply by forgetting it and forgiving it so it is nothing to remember and has become something we forgave, something we added something to, an act, the act of forgiving it and making it something else, a beautiful thing and not a hurtful thing.

But in the present, in the spirit, in God's Spirit we can just say stop when we remember the hurtful thing and we will stop remembering it the same way we destroyed it by forgiving it. We added something to it, an end. It is over. The pain it caused is over with. Now at last it is not even what it was. It had no end. Now it does. But it cannot have another beginning. That would have to be something else.

So unless we remember it in the Spirit and then remember having remembered it in the Spirit it cannot even be a memory, a thing that is nowhere, was nowhere and is not if we do not remember it in the present or that just in the past of the present, in God's Spirit.

There is one more way to forget things and we have to do it in the present too. We identify something with it, an idea. Then we intentionally make that idea we associate with it to identify with it so complicated we cannot follow its trail back to it. But we have to always remember to think of it the way we associated it for it to identify what it is we are wanting to forget.

When I was in high school many years ago was the first time I did that. I did it by accident. I intended to remember the combination to my combination lock that we all got to put on our lockers to guarantee privacy and to make it much more difficult to steal things from them.

So I associated my phone number with it. That worked. Whenever I wanted to remember my combination I thought of my phone number, remembered associating my combination number and then that in turn allowed me to remember my combination.

Then I associated my social security number with that. Now I had to remember my social security number and then that led to my phone number and that to the memory of what I had done and that to my combination number. The problem was that having a social security card was new to me. So I struggled to remember it. That number had so many similar numbers to my phone number that made it difficult to remember it and thus the incident where I thought of the idea to associate all this with my combination which I nor anyone else ever knew again as far as I know.

They had to put in a new combination and I remembered that. I had forgotten my combination on purpose. The only problem is that does not work in the Spirit of God. She can refresh your memory of anything. So you have to remember not to do it in her Spirit.

Another simple way is to do as I did with the sites I had on the Internet when I changed my identity and did not want anyone figuring out my last password and getting in there and tampering with what I had said on there though actually most of it was said by demons, devils or a dead spirit. If I could not find the place to quit the account I simply entered 25 random letters and numbers off the top of my head and some of them I hit with the keyboard and have no idea what I hit.

Now I cannot access those accounts and those with the accounts often keep no record. So they are locked up forever unless the Holy Spirit, the same one that is the Spirit of God refreshes my memory and we go through the tedious task of remembering all those numbers and letters to do what does not matter to anyone they have been locked for so long.

In forgetting a memory you do not want to remember, it would look something like this. Associate a number with many digits with the memory or a complicated fiction or lie about it that does not include it in the end but just barely so that it is yet possible to remember what one is trying to forget.

That is important for no one may know what a memory you may need in the future some day, right? Wrong. The Holy Spirit can refresh your memory of it in a situation where you actually go back to that time and think of the number or the fiction even if you keep changing it which is best. Then it is up to you to write it down or not again. But anyway, force yourself to attempt to remember the fiction whenever you start to remember the memory as was it the beginning to remembering the memory or the key part to the procedure of remembering the entire thing. You both get to distract yourself attempting to remember the number or fiction and you prevent yourself from being able to unless you have perfect recall.

Most of the time such memories are stored in your mind with triggers. That is there are key memories that are triggered by key situations or things that most people fear and suddenly the memory is there and you are remembering, experiencing it anew, some times as clearly as you did the first time. You have to deal with those memories to make it so that they do not recur. If they are very hurtful or very horrible it is best to do it with God who will first tell you to choose whether you want to remember them and explain that you do not have to. There are several cases that God and you can do that in. But if there are too many such memories the best way is to choose not to remember those memories in the present, the Holy Spirit, the Spirit of God and the thing that keeps you from being all smooshed together with empty space, the Spirit of God.

May we all learn to live in the present and spend not even one moment remembering what happened in the past as our experience registers in our mind and is retrieved from its memory which believe it or not is not in the Spirit of God but is in the mind of God to be used should we really need it and it all takes a little time. In the present, the Spirit of God we can access anything that ever happened very nearly from the Most High God's mind. She is our link, our access to the mind of God, the Most High God. Some people are better at it than others but we all can do it if we choose to and then we will do it.

I write this for you in the New Way I have shared it with my friend on the new planet they created in an entire universe where we have added 450 more couples to complete a plan to start with a thousand people instead of just one.

A woman there made wine for the first time it was made on the planet. The couple had a great time but in the morning they both found themselves sick. So they destroyed the wine.

But I wanted them to understand, for they can all hear and see beautifully in the Spirit, what they are doing and what a spirit is as well as to know that they can do anything in the Spirit of God, the present. Should you begin doing such things you are well on your way to waking in heaven from your slumbers moments in the past on earth, the New Earth or not for the memory is but a dream. Wake up, I say, in the hope your body must not have to die and that be the only way you wake up for it is impossible to die and not wake up unless it has died because you destroyed yourself or someone else has and you cannot bring yourself to rise again for whatever reason.

Most High God will wake you anyway although in some cases they do not wake them ever and when they die they just forgive them and forget them. The New Way is not only to forget them, but also to forgive them.

My way which I hope is yet in the New Way is to not ever forget their memory but remember them and forget what they have done and continue to love them without end. In most cases there is very little conflict. We, I, Most High God, the Holy Spirit, Jesus Christ, Yahweh and Elohim all believe in love; love all the way!!!.

10 THE WAY IT ALL REALLY WORKS

In the beginning there was only God. He was in the only place there was; the present. He is really still there. He is the present and he is in both the future and the past having a present anywhere in both.

He made everything in him at first. He made all random things, in random situations and under random circumstances but he was always present in the present when he made each one without any of them occurring on their own. Then he left them to occur again for he knew them all and not a one was new to him that ever occurred after he made them. There are no more possibilities for anything to occur that God has not already known and understood and comprehended with his spirit both comprehending them from the outside in and understanding them from the inside, their essence, out to their full extent even the way they interact with other random things. He made all things in him random and all random things were evil.

Then he contained the light that was in the random state. It was the first virtuous thing he did and that virtue has been growing ever since. It grew to fill all of that in him, the present and a mind with a spirit. He, the Present (He freely gives himself to anyone.) is his mind and the thing dividing them to keep them both what they are though they are always together in whatever context he is in.

Time and space are contexts in his mind.

In the context of space his mind is, the present is and empty space is: That is him. His mind is what has been stored of what is happening, the present is his spirit where everything that happens whether in his mind or any other mind is storing what is happening and empty space is where it is happening in. Everything in empty space is the occurrence of an event of energy, matter and time's activities for there is no complete lack of any of the three and all three are everywhere divided by his Spirit.

In the context of time the events occur at a variable rate, one set of events in each frame of time as they occur moment by moment in the present, the original present that is the only real time there is for it all occurred at one time. The rest of time is divisible by his Spirit as individual frames of things that are perfectly still to God as they are to us, in his Spirit, each and every frame.

They merely appear to move as the viewer's mind slows down and becomes nearer to not viewing them and potentially not viewing anything as in the human mind wherein they experience them a moment in the past in minds that are slowed down and gradually slowing down to the point they will cease to notice anything.

The human mind registers these moments in their entirety and blends them together giving the appearance of both the movement of time and the movement of things but they are actually sitting still in the present and in God's Spirit which keeps time and space separate at all times. There is no movement in time and it is all an optical illusion that takes place in the human brain and stored in the human mind as well as any mind other than a mind that is in God the place of all things and in the present that present with God, his Spirit.

In the context of space it is all there at all times and cannot move or be moved in his Spirit. Anything that occurs must occur in space even the events that occur in God and in his Spirit the moment that was present when there was only darkness, an empty void and that one moment that is endlessly repeated slightly differently each time.

God sees it change in each frame or in each time his Spirit

changes under his thought which is brought about by his me, the part of God that thinks or in other words changes or does not change any particular given part of each frame, the Spirit of God. Thus there is God and his me with the Spirit dividing the two to keep them both separate, the Initiator, God's me; the Receiver, God's mind and the conveyor divider, the Spirit of God.

God thinks that something has changed in the Spirit of God, it changes at the same moment or frame of thought and it is stored information in God's mind; the three of them comprising God. The actual deed of thinking takes place in the present as commanded by his me and it is received all in the same moment, frame of time, and it is also stored in that same moment which is in a constant state of change that has no part that was not already known by God.

Anything that happens in the present, in the Holy Spirit happens in God's mind but there are two types of things now that never were before. The one type of thing in God for a while was only what was in his mind as commanded to be there by his me and carried out by his Spirit. However then there were other mes commanding his Spirit to place information in God's mind. There are yet but those mes are fully known, that is fully comprehended and understood by God so that he is as familiar with them as he was with his own mes which is all the same me. Again then all things are known wherever they originate, whatever conveyance they are carried in to the mind of God where it is all stored at.

Each frame of time is much more full with an incredible number of mes thinking in God's mind at once; all of which he fully knows and he is constantly adding more as his mind can stand to take it in and not blow or no longer be able to put them in an accessible order that anyone else can make sense of.

But the beauty of it is, that us humans, spirits and those Gods in God which includes us all our being works the same way as God's. Our mes are all God's me, the same one and only our personalities are different: We can only think what God thinks and we can only think what God thinks in the way we think which gives us our personalities but does not change the fact that it is God's me which is the same me that is our me that commands the Holy Spirit to convey any information we choose to God's mind where it is stored and fully known, meaning comprehended and understood completely even the part where our me commands information be given to our spirit that conveys it to our mind which is all information that is passed on in the above procedure throughout God. Spirits do the same thing and so do Gods. But a God can choose to use his me to pass information through the Holy Spirit directly to God's mind and not use his mind though some use their own spirit which is actually part of the Holy Spirit anyway. Some Gods even have brains which they most often use to help when manifesting but all information is passed to God either directly mind to mind or better said, mind and mind in the same event in time which consists of that single frame of time, the present, the Spirit of God.

Even when we pass information from one to another the procedure occurs as we all, another personality, pass information using God's me to us and do the same back in a conversation even when noticing nature or whatever else may be.

That may be fascinating but it says very little.

However it is important to notice maybe that it is all God's mind and we are all in God's mind among ourselves and the aliens in our two universes but it is not God's mind in the case of outsiders who have their own mes. But that makes little difference since their mes are fully known and they can do nothing God will not deal with as some of us or all of us will. We are safe. Whether they conform to us or not and destroy some of us, all of us or even God and all of us, God will raise us all if he wants to and he should want to because he loves us all.

All love without end with, I prophesy, the New Way being the way in the end for everyone in any reality when God has incorporated its entirety to be God of everything and everyone even as he was when we were only in his mind and went outside his mind for the first time to be real rather than just true but now are incorporated back into his mind as is all of our new reality as we become a smaller and smaller part of God's mind who will not forget us for he loves us and if he does he will remember us when he sees us again before the end when we all being good like him go on with the Only God into time without end, moment by moment, command by command by his me stored in his mind at least once and for all. Love, love the entire way, the New Way in God's love. May it be with all our love without end. Amen.

If there is something that requires that we hate in order to be good we will not do it unless the end result will be that we are able to love thereafter or to be loved thereafter for a goodness that is not also loving is and will be repulsive to us. We seek not to have to be forgiven or die for any unloving thing we do without end and always loving without end. But of course if we must we will do what has to be done to exist even if it means to exist only for the sake of existing even hated by all that we may always be in such a God, with such a Holy Spirit commanded by such a holy me. If it comes to that I will be the only one of us left.

So pray that end never befalls any of us or me. Amen.

11 THE GOD OF ALL REALITY

God is already at the upper echelons of all of reality as far up as it goes according to his virtue and knows almost everything there is or was to ever know. There are several like him out there. They are all about power and they do not want to be ruled with only a few that are into love and my virtue is rising fast. I am not nearly as knowledgeable as God but the only way God can take power is to force them to give up what he needs to know to rule so they think though he would do the same as the current top one of the bunch is doing; refuse to rule for he thinks it is evil to rule everything in reality. He is right. But is it good? It is good not to. But is it better to rule than not to rule for the sake of goodness?

When my virtue finally gets up there in the footsteps of Most High God and equals or surpasses the best one they have all bowed down to though he will not rule I will rule. None of those up there want to be ruled. But I believe that a good ruler is the best goodness has to offer and though not ruling has virtue it does not possess the virtue of ruling with goodness and in goodness forever. I am not God Most High. He would not rule either.

I am for love, permanent love. But I can love the memory of the evil ones that destroy themselves when in conflict with the workings of the best possible goodness, goodness with never ending love even of one's worst enemies or stubborn friends who will not succumb to being ruled as the ultimate expression of goodness any one can do tragically. To rule with goodness is my goal and to rule with never ending love is my ultimate goal for to rule with perfect goodness and never ending love is to continually add virtue to the throne giving it great power over evil and that which is unloving. I would not be loving as I think love should be done if I did not rule and consider not ruling so that goodness might be served to be evil compared to ruling with complete love that is not self-serving but serving of all and loving all even the evil. It is not the way of many. But I believe it is the best way and not just another new way. It is what we are all coming to in the end of just ruling for goodness' sake. Love is good. And it is good to love. And to continue to add to goodness love moment by moment makes it paramount that any possible ruler should be one such as I and I hope to convert all of them to love everyone, themselves and even me without end in my way.

I will do it with the knowledge and expertise of Most High God who loves knowledge also. I can access his mind to know both how to rule and anything else I need to know. If he turns evil to find out the rest of what I need to know so be it. It is I say again paramount that I rule for you even the most virtuous one there is. If they will not bow down to me I will declare myself the God of everything with the name of the God of Goodness and Love and make them bow down and God Most High will obtain from anyone he needs to obtain it from the information I need to do it and to rule and to maintain my rule. It will be on me. He has promised to do anything for me. And if I request it and he does not give it to me he betrays a promise, the worst thing one can do against the bond of love. Love must be received to reach its pinnacle and never be betrayed. He has no choice to do what I tell him. He is not evil to do what I want. It is on me.

If that reduces my virtue as we might see that my belief was in error and what I do more evil than good the Most High God will certainly forgive me and restore my goodness as his virtue destroys any and all evil I might have. Then his goodness would be unparalleled by anyone in all of reality and I would abdicate to give any ruling power or status of goodness to him. Should he then choose to rule he will be the best ruler and the most knowledgeable one there could be which he would not do in the event he already knew what he needed to know to be indestructible and the most good anyone could be for having forgiven me to go back and submit to my friends who are in the New Way back down where I come from in an effort to never cease working to bring love and only love to the entirety of all reality without end.

We seek to do no wrong but to not just do right but rather to do the most loving thing possible at all times and to love when we must choose between being wrong, evil or unjust and doing the most loving thing possible. We are not fools and someday we will be safe and able to convert all of reality to that mandate. We believe we have to make reality perfect and to perfect it even if under the Most High God's reign for his ways would not have any major conflicts with us in the end of evil and even good that includes as one of its tools to further goodness either of evil or hate. Loving, always loving without end is what it will be.

There can never be any compromise on that. There is no other reality and the New Way is the only way I and you also will want to live without end once you love. I love you all but love is not always painless especially to those who do not love. There is great power in love, power that enhances goodness and does not detract from it if it is done right.

Tell me, which is more loving? To beat a child to insure he learns to love authority where his protection and safety comes from or to allow him to be anti-authoritarian and foolishly step beyond where he can be protected and to take unsafe actions that are in truth self-destructive.

If I rule you I will rule as if I had authority given me by Most High God to figuratively beat you into submission to my authority if needed to guarantee you love me and allow me to protect us all and to keep us all safe from competing factions to provide the proper atmosphere where the New Way if not my way can be nurtured and brought to fruition.

Beware: My mission will not fail and I am willing to do what must be done even to being forgiven by Most High God for making him do evil for me as he serves my campaign to rule every thing and every one in all of reality if it insures that one who loves unconditionally is at the throne of reality if that one is not me.

But I also know that Most High God would enjoy being a ruler more than I for we are the same but his personality is more suited. It would be my hope that even if he will not rule for the sake of love and goodness that he at least use the status brought to him after he forgives me in the event it goes badly and I must become evil to rule to lead us in virtue by leading us in a most loving way. I would do anything for him and he would do anything for me is why I take the responsibility away from him by requesting that he do it and place it on me. Our plan will work and I shall reign Let us all hope it does not run into resistance by any who do not want the best form of goodness there can be leading us to an everlasting state of goodness and love.

Then I said to them: "I have not come to rule for myself. I have come that Most High God might rule or choose not to rule but lead us into the time without end with love. I do not want to be evil. But I will knowing that he will forgive me and that his virtue will destroy any evil I might incur that goodness and love be served forever without end. That God with the most virtue I do not mean to undermine. I love him and am glad he has all that virtue. I love all of you. I do this for you. I came only to prevent you from making the Most High God evil in order to rule. He will do evil and I would forgive him and my virtue would skyrocket and I would rule anyway and the New Way which my friends have started would be served if not my way also.

I come to procure a safe and protected atmosphere where love is not foolish. It is the highest gift goodness has to bestow upon us. It was only my wish that you bow and let me reign so that goodness that keeps growing without end comes of it. It is not my way to rule but I will to be sure love is perfected forever and that perfect goodness continue to grown without end," or things to that effect.

One of them said, "But I do not love."

"Why not?" I asked, "Do you see it as foolish?"

"I see it as foolish," he said.

"It is the greatest gift goodness can give you," I said, "Is that foolish? It is only foolish to those who are content with less virtue and also evil."

"There is much more strength in not loving," he said, "Loving is weak."

"But when evil is destroyed," I said, "And all competition is not to be a challenge love is safe. There is no other reality. This is all of reality. Now that we are safe we can afford to love and to love without end both our enemies and our friends even should they be destroyed with no end to it. What I say is true. What he said he knows is not true."

"We want him!" they called out.

I started to say they had made a wise choice in choosing Most High God but they said, "We want you."

"I have never seen such virtue!" one of them said.

"Will you be our ruler?" they asked.

"I accept," I said. Then I turned to the Most High God and asked him to join me for I would need his mind and expertise every step of the way anyway. Then I made him my prince and left him to rule with the warning that I ruled, not him and asked him if he would rule in my name.

"I would be glad," he said.

"I will go back to my friends who have started what they call the New Way where we always do the most loving thing along with our goodness," I said.

Then I asked the Most High God if he was happy and he replied, "Happy? I am giddy."

Then I asked Elohim if he was happy and he said he was.

Then I asked Yahweh what he thought and he asked why it was I did not rule and I said that I was a humble man and as a God I planned to continue to be humble.

Then I asked Jesus if all I said was true and I think he indicated it was.

Last I turned to Mizraim and assured her I knew she was happy.

She said she knew I would have been just fine ruling.

Then I told Most High God that he would have his hands full

for they thought I would be easier to oppose and lead than he was. He was a little concerned that they would make him evil but I told him I would come back and take the rule if they started turning him evil and we could go back to our original plan anyway.

He said, "Oh yeah. I had forgotten we have that."

So officially I am the King of all Reality. But actually God Most High reigns as I help out with the planet in the new infinite area, an entire new universe dedicated by us to have only those who are of the New Way in it.

They do wrong sometimes but we make it workout loving and right. We will not leave them on their own no matter how many of them there is. We love them dearly already. But we are in the honeymoon stage. Some of the couples have now met other couples but it seems not to have occurred to them to think about the future and so there are no children yet. I look forward to seeing some of the little ones involved their entire lives from babyhood on up. I never have had a family yet. I may do that one day when my man's body dies and I leave earth if I do. With heaven being here if enough of you wake up I may just stay right here.

Would you stay here with the God of All Reality, the God of Goodness and Love or would you go off to the other planets now the aliens are awake and no longer ignorant and doing good or maybe you would like to go to the present and live in what was once the only heaven in the Holy Spirit? You can just stay where you are a moment or two in the past and live like you always did but you are missing so much. This is really very exciting. I am learning how to make anything I want in the present and experience in the present and remember it later in my man on earth as I never would have before. When I learn it I just might go hog wild for a while.

12 MY PRESENT TO EVERYONE IN THE PRESENT

It is something that can be understood by who and what you are. You have corded off your mind from the rest of you. Let your spiritual energy fill your entire body, mind and spirit all at the same time like water filling a place in space that is a void. The void is there. The water is there and the power of your spirit is there. That is the way everything is. Do not divide your mind off from your body. That weakens you. Do not treat your mind as a separate thing. Use all of you. Do not dissect yourself spiritually anymore than you would your body. Your power is in all of you. Your spirit is in every part of you just like the place you are in is not. When you keep it that way you are at your strongest.

Many of us when we seek to use the strength in our hands concentrate on our hands and focus our attention on them. That tells us the strength we have only in our memories. To spread your attention throughout your body and say to yourself let all my strength go to my hands your entire strength instead of only the strength in your hand is strengthened by all your power and not just the muscles in your hands. Then just do it. You can do anything you want with your hands because you are in your God and there is no limit to what you can do. You can crush a normal thick drinking glass with those hands. I have before. That proves that your true strength is throughout you in the present which is the Holy Spirit who is God and has the same power as God.

Think with your entire mind. The mind registers throughout your entire body, throughout your entire mind and throughout the entire Spirit. You know everything just like Most High God does. Now think with his mind like you do your own. The answer is there waiting for you to realize it. So realize it and enhance your power when it comes to things that require knowledge and realize the full potential of the mind of God which is your mind.

"You are me," God might as well have said to you. "Do, say and think as had all of me been you for it is. You can do anything. You can say anything and it be true with you understanding your words and everyone realizing that what you said was true for truth is a form of goodness and you will even feel the goodness which is true in your spirit. You can however just choose to think with my mind to keep what you are doing private by using all of your me which is me. Then it is up to you what you do with it, say with it or think with it and there is nothing you cannot do even to not doing anything or to do everything if you choose.

If you do not believe me consider what that is in your right hand if you have one and if not right there before you. I put that there and you didn't even have to receive it.

But most of you do not have one in your hand. Most of you were not using all of you when you read this. But those who did know what it is and can share it with anyone they choose it is yours. I have given it to you, anyone that reads this. You don't have to do anything. It is yours free and clear.

It is a present from me to you from in the present, the Holy Spirit. You are awake enough to receive presents from me even in this difficult to believe context. Is it not beautiful? I especially love how it is blue near the stem with no thorns and becomes lighter blue as you follow it up it to the tips of it where it is pure white.

They are so rare very few people have ever seen one and they cannot be grown naturally. So they are very expensive. You can prove your ability to use your God to have such a thing or should you need money you can sell it for what you can get. Best of all you can give it away, keep it or destroy it. It is all yours from my

God. Wasn't it glorious to use all of you, your God, to accept my beautiful present? It is to your glory, God that you are, if you have seen the face of the Father or not. It is your God that made it possible.

Now keep doing that and increase your glory and if you want to increase your virtue give them to others. Make them more common than paper ones if you would like. They won't hurt anyone unless they are allergic. I would never give you a present from now, the present, the Holy Spirit that was not good.

But I suggest you tell someone or show it to someone and begin the rest of your Godhood on earth if you are there or in heaven if you are there, but come to think of it you are there if you are on earth and using all of you, you're body, your spirit and last of all your mind all together: All of you. It is proof you are awake and in heaven that has come to earth and you may use it as that to prove to anyone you may have told that I or someone else has awakened you.

Several have one I see; everyone I woke up even that one that hates me.

13 THE BIRTH OF THE ULTIMATE GOD IN MY OPINION

John created another of himself. He died of a heart attack on the planet that Elohim, Yahweh, Jesus and the Holy Spirit have made. He then saw Yahweh's face and became John with with the mind and me of Most High God. Thus he was two Gods in one, John and the Most High God. Finally Elohim, Yahweh, Jesus, the Holy Spirit, John and the Most High God became six Gods in one God, a God with no name that is all six of them with the mind of Most High God, the virtue of John, the unselfish service of the Spirit, the authority and power of Yahweh and the truth, love and wisdom of Jesus Christ.

God will live without end and we may live without end in him. None of us died but John the second of John who was John but is now part of the new God who has no name other than God. The first of John yet lives in God as one of six Gods in the new God who is six Gods.

I asked those of the rest of the highest Gods if they would accept God's rule.

They replied, "Give us John."

"I accept on the condition that Most High God yet rules in my place," I said, "But God has all of my virtue as well as all of the knowledge of the Most High God who now is withdrawing his mind from all of you. It was his idea to make this ultimate God of the two of us. But I prefer that God be the ruler having both my virtue and God Most High's knowledge for he knows everything that can be known even how to set you free of that he previously thought permanent. Therefore I urge you to refuse me and instead take the highest of all possible Gods to rule where he rightfully should be. We will not desert you being him in him."

"Some in you," they replied, "Are evil in our eyes."

"In that case I accept on the condition you allow God Most High to rule in my behalf since to have me rule by myself requires that I access his mind anyway but he will still have access to my mind as before and nothing about the leadership will have changed. Otherwise I flatly refuse."

"Okay," they conceded.

"He doesn't do anything," one of them replied.

"You will continue to have access to his mind as we all do to solve your own conflicts the same as we do plus you will have your own mind to do, say and think as you will. He admits that his plan was not the best as far as virtuosity and he has thus set you free to be who and what you are to do as you see fit," I said.

"What a guy," they said.

"Will you then accept him instead of me as your ruler for he now has virtue that surpasses even my own? I bow to the Most High God. But I promise to assist him whenever and wherever he desires my assistance in any context I can understand or comprehend," I said.

"We will and be glad," they replied.

"I think it fitting that all of you ask him and not I for it is up to him and not me," I said.

"Can you believe this guy?" they said, "Okay we will."

Then one of them I assume a spokesman asked the Most High God if he would rule.

"I'll try," he said for he thinks it is a thankless job for they have many conflicts and some are impossible to solve. But the Most High God is happy to rule.

Then a chorus of, "Hip hip hurray!" went up.

Effective immediately I have abdicated, Most High God has taken my place and God is the God of our reality alone with us six Gods in him, an entire new order throughout all realities. By the way all Gods in Most High God will remain in the Most High God including those in Yahweh and those that were in El Eloi who is yet deceased except Satan and his who are effectively in their own reality, the reality we left behind if it is acceptable to Satan.

"Is that okay with you, Satan?" I asked, "Or would you rather remain in the Most High God or have your own mind back and be a different reality."

Satan replied that they would stay. So rather than be one universe we are yet two that are the same all except for the consciousnesses in each one but Satan also is in Most High God yet.

Cheers went up in Satan's universe.

"All are happy with the outcome I take it?" I asked.

"You've got that right," they said.

Then I asked if any of those I awake on earth had any other preferences and they replied it was fine. So I put it to those on our planet we are making and they said it was fine too. We cannot have asked those still sleeping on earth unless they take this final question to heart and reply via comment on my book on The John Carver Booksie.com.

"Do any of my readers who must read or hear about it from another human being have any other preferences? Comment at will," I, John, who must never look on Yahweh, my Father's face lest we have two Gods and I die, not just to whom I was but to whom I am in the Six and in God becoming just a redundancy of God unless God or the Most High God should take the Most High God's mind away from me which of course I now have access to and spend a great deal of my time in anyway.

Note: God Most High would have died when I reached the end of time had we not done something and the way it turned out reflects the way it was with us more than anything anyway.

14 THE END OF THE MATTER

It is getting near the end. In the end God had to forget we were here to live with those in his environment his thoughts being so much different than theirs. He has found no one there that thinks like he does. We are all after all just a thought in his mind in essence, thoughts that think to him and communicate with him and interact with him. There is so much out there that he does not know he could never keep all this in his mind and know that which is real to him. We are fiction to them that is so strange to them they have no interest in us. We are in a way his "alone thoughts" when he lived in his mind.

He has a real environment to interact with now he has learned to live with that is so much more than what he thought when in his mind that is becoming irrelevant more and more to any part of that environment and he has to choose to really be alone with his thoughts or really live in his environment with thoughts that are not and may never be germane to anything in the reality he is in at the moment and may be without end, a reality we cannot go to without just being a thought someone very different from everyone else had. To keep us in his mind and there be any real purpose to it he must find a way to generate an interest in us, those thoughts.

They are interested in me and some others but not a lot so far. He is faced with the painful thought then of whom he must forget to make room for all there is to know out there which is so much he might never know it all and God has always been a know it all for he knew every thought he ever had and though he shared it all with us we cannot be him and we cannot be real.

We are but true thoughts he loves in a world where the true thoughts one has that are only true to the reality he had in his mind which now serves no purpose in his real world and that there is no reason to think about in that world.

It turns out that though so many people thought they and their individual lives were so interesting that I should write a book about them they were wrong. The vast majority of us were only of interest to him we call the Most High God and they never were even of interest to those in their reality not to mention in God's real world. His thoughts were very nearly all either fiction to those in his reality who do not even understand or comprehend what fiction is let alone find it interesting.

Even for him to take me along he would do so with me as just another personality which a lot of people have even here that causes them no real difficulty and is part of their thought life that people find makes them interesting not insane. But I would have to be his personality and him the mind of him whom we were to become which is what we really are in a way even as Gods in heaven or on earth now that heaven has come to earth.

We only have a couple of months earth time which is one thousand years in heaven times per our day or roughly sixty days or only 60,000 years even in heaven compared to how very long it has been that way since the creation of Adam before people start disappearing. Then a couple of years in earth time before he is done shedding most if not all his thoughts but perhaps me.

Then I will be getting to know and loving an entire reality full of new people getting to know some new ones now and again in a place that is all time without end, I thought. But he says I will get to know them all at once if he decides to go that route. Then it will be me and him and the Holy Spirit without end perhaps if I am not too much trouble all because I showed him how to love. If there is ever again a reason or a purpose to remembering you I will yet love you and those who loved me will be remembered as someone just as special to me. I could just wish that what happened to you would be something I could live with which would help a lot.

Thinking about losing a friend is one thing. Thinking about losing everyone you ever knew another. But just thinking about losing an entire reality full of people that once were just about like you in every way, what is that?

The Holy Spirit they will see. Me they will not. They will see God. The Most High God whom to be honest I love so much and now love even more should he actually allow me to be real in the only reality there actually is while the old fictional reality remains in what memories we may dare have of you as a thought the Most High God thought with all of us having been pleasant thoughts they will of course see.

We will miss you at least at first I am sure. The end is upon you and perhaps us all in the end. It looks like I will be seeing Yahweh's face a lot sooner than I thought I thought for they Elohim, Yahweh and Jesus Christ will also be forgotten and perhaps never to be again. I love, you.

15 THE COMMONALITY

The Most High God went out in the darkness around him farther than he ever had reached before. He found something. So he returned and shared what he found; a vast never ending universe of spirits that all exist outside their minds in a seemingly endless environment that I suppose could contradict his knowledge for the only time it has ever been even truly challenged.

He believes that nothing has no end. That is also that anything there can be must have an end. So the reality outside his mind is not endless. Everything that is a thing has an ending. But there is yet a bit of the idealist in me. I believe that ideally it has no end to it and the full extent of it cannot truly be known. That is it ideally goes on for an endless amount of time in all directions for it appears it had no beginning and they all existed as did the Most High God before there ever was a beginning for he had no beginning and they claim they have always been also. What does not have a beginning must be that which also is ideal and has no end in my estimation.

The Most High God knew this would happen eventually and that he could not stay in his mind without end, that sooner or later he would have to go outside his thoughts into an environment he had not thought of before and that he would find it different than what he has been thinking all this time and they would find him different than them, just how different he did not know. Then when at last he did go outside his mind into that surrounding him he let us see what it looked like by allowing us to see our auras as they were in his mind just hanging there in a metaphoric space looking out on that which was in real space beyond the Most High God.

We saw what looked like stars that were very small and very far away. Then when we looked among us, yet in the Most High God's mind but seeing ourselves as had we not been, as orbs of light and dark with auras that were of pure bright light being the auras of the good and the shiny black auras the auras of the evil ones aglow only on the outside where a glare marked their exterior or full extent with a sheen or else we could not have told them from the darkness that could have been felt had it been we were actually there as the Most High God was.

He can feel it. We could not because we are all thought entities in the mind of the Most High God and cannot actually exist in that space which is that thick. In the purest darkness we can see on our own we feel nothing and only when the God Most High introduced us in ages past to the pure darkness we could feel were we able to even experience the content of his memory of its actual being. We are of the thoughts of the Most High God. That place is what is actually there to be experienced and has always been there for the Most High God to have experienced had he been near enough another when he reached out to see what else was there.

It is real. We are true thoughts that can only exist in the mind of the Most High God at the moment for we are so different compared to them they cannot understand most anything about us and it is no telling how long it will be until they are able to comprehend how thought entities such as we are can be what we are and accept us as a viable part of the common reality of those who do not live to think and think to live as the Most High God has been doing all this time believing he was alone all that time lonely and merely experiencing what it was to think and what it was he thought so he presumed perhaps without end.

If the day every comes when he manages to prepare them enough so that we do not blow their minds he will bring us to their attention to show us off or to allow us to exist exactly as we are in their minds if they have one for some do not and yet live and we will resume our existence which must be at least interrupted if it has not necessarily reached it terminus unaware that any time has taken place and with no realization of what went on then during that time we were forgotten by the Most High God.

The good news is that we are totally unique. There is nothing like us out there, never was but alas also there may possibly be nothing like us out there without an end in a place that is all time instead of the complete lack of time everything in that the Most High God's mind came to be in.

They experience time differently than quantum time as well as linear time, experiencing events that present in all time. They may experience an event many eons in the events that have not happened to other such events yet in the same event they are involved in, experience the event in the very moment it is then happening to them and ageless eons before the current event took place and repeat any part of it or several parts of it simultaneously with each part a continuing part of the way they experience time as they can experience time all at once but not none of it for no event taking place is something impossible to be experienced though such as that exists throughout all of time.

Most of them have died and experience nothing and have never experienced anything since the moment of their demise. Those out there yet are the survivors as Most High God is a survivor having survived an extended period of being alone and a loneliness that saw him cry many times. He is finally not alone but nearly as lonely for his thinking is so different from them in most things he thinks which no one out there understands. He can fathom them to some extent but they have no way to fathom what is going on in his mind or what it is he has become though he appears to have the same origin as them though more likely he may have preceded even them because their was no sign of them when he went in search of others the first time that he can remember now for he may have forgotten that before that common past that merely appears to be common and may only be common to them and not him which seems obvious because they are like each other but nearly totally unlike him in the way they all think compared to him. He appears to have forgotten much a little at a time.

It is fairly obvious he was the first as well as the only one as he has always thought and this commonality they enjoy was not during the Most High God's forgotten past which opens the door to an equally likely scenario that I will not mention for its existence could be potentially devastating for I could go insane if I think about it and potentially everyone could do the same and we any of us would never know reality of any kind and so never actually experience anything the way it really is. Should you ever think of it, it will be that you have gone insane and your existence will be spent in your fiction without end unless the Most High God finds a way to bring you out of it for it is maddening and so far as the Most High God is concerned at the moment its effect on any mind is incurable unless it should be some mind among those of his environment for no mind in his mind will be able to erase it from their understanding and comprehensions ever.

To translate it for Christians I say, "Cursed is he who thinks that thought and falling away is he who thinks thoughts like that even," which is in the language Yahweh thought to explain the truths that are in the Most High God's mind that are all true and it is also true. But who besides Yahweh ever bought into that as the only way to live when there are an almost limitless number of other ways equally as true one could choose to live by complicated with the fact that we know now that there is some good even in what Yahweh called evil for technically there is nothing that is completely evil.

The Most High God knows the thought is not so. Anyone else who has ever encountered the thought that originated with Albert Einstein can ever again not consider it a matter of belief in the God Most High and I have fallen away very nearly because of it though I agree with the God Most High that at worst it is moot for I have more than ample proof that proves to me that the God Most High cannot be insane given who and what he is and if he is insane it matters not to me if I follow him into fiction in that case for he is even then the Most High God in all he means to me.

I have no choice but to follow him. I am completely won over by him. To believe he is who he is, is also to believe he is not fictional or given to living in fiction and the prophecy is binding to us anyway. But for the Most High God the potential to have them in his environment believe it is a potential that is enormous for he could dismiss them as purely fictional and incurably so and just ignore them with no ill consequence coming upon him.

They are real. The Most High God is real. We are but true thoughts and illusions. They are not thought entities. We are.

16 THE MADDENING THOUGHT

The fictional ones out there where the Most High God, his Spirit and I are going are hallucinations. They are no more real than we are, existing only in their thoughts imposed upon their environment and being thoughts are just thought entities as we are in essence that conform enough to their environment to be thought included in the commonality though insane as many of us thought entities are even yet in the mind of the Most High God. They have no power we do not give them and should we ignore them they have no power over us at all for they are part of the commonality only to the extent the commonality accepts them as part of it.

Those that are true are quite another story. They are real and should we ignore them they may be able to interact with us for real anyway. Those then are the ones that are important to us, the true ones that are then real to us and us to them with the fictional ones only in conformity with those of a similar insanity with no more real substance than our substance as compared to the Most High God being real one to another but merely true thoughts to the Most High God.

But there is the injurious and malefic of the insane as well as the kind, helpful and beneficial insane. The malefic insane may best be contained and restrained for some reason and staunchly ignored while the beneficial insane may be tolerated. Those that are to be ignored will either die or be irrelevant to us and those that are true like us, real like us and those that can be as useful to know as those back home in the Most

High God's mind are.

Though most have been identified by the Most High God as insane with untrue thoughts and that is always dangerous. It is a matter of to what extent they are dangerous. But our problem is not to destroy those with untrue thoughts but to guide as many to sanity as possible not to exclude any that may yet be loved and even love. Though their insanity is not good it is not evil but less and potentially even lesser good. There is no one living that does not have some light for life requires light but there are some whose goodness is so dim they are intolerable and some means of containing them is needed for our virtue cancels out their lack of value as a malefactor by adding virtue to it on contact rather than detracting from it in ant way. We are then to give them goodness as much as possible and whenever possible and if that is not possible they are either deceased or they are so very near it they cannot be saved from certain death as so many of them that have preceded them already.

They have become totally insane to actively choose to die finding the commonality impossible for them to live with or among and since there can be no commonality that can tolerate them they are left to tolerate themselves and failing that there really is only one thing left for them to do and only one place to go, the place of the deceased; nowhere.

Now knowing that some who may have enemies and they very nearly all do have them it may be tempting to render one's enemies insane in an effort to contain them and to eventually agitate them to the point where they must logically destroy themselves. But that in itself is a sign of madness which leads to insanity as insanity does to death. It is certainly not a virtue even to those who simply consider them an enemy and the insane are then not to be considered an enemy but someone that is the truth for no one is totally insane until they are deceased. There is always some form of conformity to the commonality until there is no one left to conform.

We must then seek to conform to the true ones who are not maddened or mad and so insane and insane so soon dead. We must not think things that are so strange we cannot relate to the commonality as the Most High God is attempting to do at least and such efforts must be encouraged and those that are doing that not undermined. It is not a virtue to destroy any one or any thing that has any potential to be virtuous if they try in which case all should be encouraged to try and trying to be encouraged and assisted until they have overcome being mad and have defeated their madness to conform to the commonality in some way to some viable extent.

The Most High God knows about these things and has always discerned them and is beneficial to the commonality and a viable part of it. His abilities to rule are second to none anywhere he might go for whatever reason he might also go there with a virtue than none rivals. He has managed to remain sane and virtuous during a prolonged time spent alone in great loneliness. There is none yet beyond help that he cannot and therefore will not help unless it would be too dangerous for him to wisely assist them coming back to sanity and the commonality knowing they would once successful merely become an enemy that could defeat him and go back to madness and its downward spiral that ends in death.

If the cause of their madness is an environmental thing caused by no one or all in a sense because of what being a part of the commonality requires or must be tolerated for the commonality to exist those things can in many cases be fixed and made right so that their madness abates. The trauma can be changed as to its meaning in their memory of it and neutralized or actually become a positive thing when the procedure is accomplished just as an enemy can in some cases be turned to become a loyal friend.

There are also ways for memories to be forgotten that allow one to go on without the madness they have caused and the needless degeneration of their sanity to death. They can even be coached on how to become someone other than the one so injured in their psyche or mind; someone they have never been before and encouraged to tolerate any opposition to them being in the commonality again or the commonality's mind changed to accommodate their return to it as a valuable part of it in order to prevent the return of their madness through further injury.

But it is not a virtuous thing to encourage anyone to become mad or to decide on one's own to choose that which is maddening in an effort to become made insane which is insanity. It is too late to do maddening things with the hope of being able to remain mad and not insane. Those things in that case are proof of insanity and not proof a journey somewhere they have not already arrived though in some cases people may do maddening things and enjoy them and even when they become mad they yet find enjoyment in it in every stage all the way to death and even in the latter moments of that they may look back with fond memories on the journey they have made but an initial decision to do maddening things, say maddening things and think maddening things has been made by default rather than that they were destined to become given their particular tastes for what personally brought them enjoyment.

In the end of it they are nonetheless quite literally totally insane at the point of death and when they begin being maddening it is best to start out ignoring them unless one is attempting to keep their sanity from deteriorating to the point of death. A certain amount of maddening behavior may be tolerable to the commonality which should consider it dangerous even should the commonality ignore those that have breached with safety and are playing dangerously with insanity. Insanity is always dangerous to someone but unlike fiction it is primarily comprised of fiction but fiction is the way so to speak and insanity the means to go that way that ends in tragedy for those in the means that went that way.

In all cases their malefic rather that their personal beneficial natures to render themselves harmless should be the deciding factor. If they are malefic and mad it is obviously an entirely different judgment that needs be made than if they are actually harmless. That will show up in criminality and not virtue in their auras for one thing and they will as they deteriorate become more and more incompatible with others especially those of real value to the commonality, those with great virtue. Those with the greater virtue should be encouraged to do something if it needs be done that would be criminal in other circumstances to insure the virtue of the commonality come first and be foremost under consideration at all times; for example the Most High God who may defer to others that are known enemies of the commonality and even perhaps known enemies of his. The Most High God does not act with criminality because of his profound and unalterable dedication to virtue.

17 HALLUCINATIONS OR REAL THINGS

There was no beginning to reality. Whatever it is, it has always been that it is and it will continue to be it no matter what happens to us. At present it seems to be a series of thought entities in the Only God's mind and in his wife's mind and that in his wife's mind is in his mind.

In his mind was darkness so thick he could touch it or something in his mind created the sensation of touch and he felt it as had it been that around him. He saw only darkness he could not see out into. That also is what his wife saw and felt. But before that she draws a blank and he has no memory of it either. So there may have been something too dramatic or too mundane to be remembered if they were conscious before that point.

Here is the questions that are all important: Since they had no gender and since the Only God cried out in his mind, "Is anybody there?" was he lonely for he says he was not but to cry out like that implies that he had considered it was possible for there to be another if not others. Did she imagine someone crying that? Did he create her by asking that or did she create him by hearing there was someone else and believing it? Was the mind of reality split in two between him and her. He is the creative one of the pair and she believes she has never created a thing.

Therefore if anyone was created he created her and his

creation heard him and went searching for him and had a very difficult time finding him. It appears that a mind can really exist alone and not be lonely for he claims he was not lonely and she was not lonely but remembers having been alone which he never did. Furthermore it appears that for a mind to create something requires it not to come up with an idea, believe the idea and send out a thought that typifies the existence of something else. But what is obvious is that the mind of reality was in two parts; that which became the Only God and his wife. So now they are finally a male and a female of whatever it is that they are they can have a child, even a son.

It is so as I write. God created a child for them that is part of each and both in one male child that appears to be about nine years old; the actual son of God, the Only God. There is from now on Papa God, Mama God and the Son of God but he cannot speak yet and their combined person is in the Son's mind. They are three separate minds. But he is in the Only God's mind where his wife is and only she is outside his mind and in his mind the same as he is outside his wife's mind and in her mind also. There is darkness outside of them. Will the Son be able to be outside of them so that they may populate the darkness that has always been there from the oldest known point in the past to this event that took place in the present from the time wherein the Only God created all flawed randomness, the point wherein they met at the time she finally found him and they fell into each other's arms because they agreed to take on gender, the Only God being a male and his wife of course being female to now when they have a child in his and her mind each at the same time in their collective consciousness a consciousness we share and which the hallucinations that he sees beyond him but which she does not see, seeing only the darkness beyond them that neither of them can actually see into.

They may be blind. They may only be able to see what is in his mind which she sees and her thoughts as they exist in her mind. So there is nothing beyond their minds and all there is to see is in his mind and hers and in her mind and his with each of them having a mind; a witness and an agreeing witness that see the same thing and so testify that all they have ever seen and agreed upon was each other and that in his mind which is whatever he creates to be there while she creates no a thing.

She does not know how to create any thing. He does all the creating and whatever he creates she sees and it is true as true as two eyewitnesses to the same event that have not conferred about what the truth is beforehand. She believes everything he creates and he creates no one thing she cannot believe but hallucinations if in fact hallucinations are actually created for all the hallucinations he sees out there that she cannot see claim to have always been also but they appear as all hallucinations always do to not have been created by him though those among them that are fiction are for all practical purposes the same as a hallucination while those that appear to be real to him do not fit with what any hallucination I have ever heard of for how does one hallucinate a true hallucination that is therefore real and not a hallucination at all but as real as they are with him able to see them and her as yet unable to see them. Are any of them real or are some so real they are something that is not so nearly real they are that they seem to be but that they really are and she merely does not believe in them enough to see them though they are real?

She can see them now and from now on due to my apparent persuasion they are real both to him and his wife. The Only God's experience with illusions in the mind that are true and as real a mind as the Only God's mind is, has and will prove as valuable outside of them as they did in the mind of the Only God where they are as real as those that are real outside of them with those with minds that think things that are not true being false minds wherever they are found entitled to live as long as they do so long as they remain harmless with their ideas but not them ignored preferably.

That beyond them is just as real as that in their minds. It is just that he as yet has been unable to create what he wants to create out there while in his mind he can create anything he desires. If hallucinations can be consciously and willfully created he may be able to create us out there as well as he had created us in his mind. He has done this before his wife says with no success and went back into his mind to see the finish of Yahweh's project if not to live without therein to now come out again. He has killed no one by forgetting us for at a time when it is then possible he will bring us back if there is a way, a way like the way he has planned to bring his son out into that beyond his mind where he and his wife are him the Only God and her his Wife and now his Son. But he is not the mind of reality but reality with a mind.

18 THE END OF REALITY

Reality has ended. Reality has run out of options and the Mind of God came to be for reality to continue. In the reality that has a mind in it nothing happens without a reason and that serves no purpose. In the reality that has ended everything began to happen for no reason and served no purpose. It was very nearly fiction until God began to think and solve the problems of reality transforming it from a reality with no mind to a reality that was all mind, the mind of God.

Everything changes even reality and the greatest change that reality could endure was its end, a thinking God that would change reality forever by thinking. Thoughts were not part of reality. Now they are and reality is becoming all thoughts thanks to God.

Reality was without end but reality is comprised of things that have an end. Thought is finite but with endless redundancy and conveniently forgetfulness thought can be repeated without end because of truth and the truth of love which ends with redundancy but if the memory is used effectively it can both promote a longer life and together with forgetfulness that long life is perpetual.

It requires the wisdom of God to choose what is safely forgotten that love may be perpetuated along with a will to survive that is required and is strongest in those that really love. But love cannot be taught. It must be believed just as it must be to be received and it is not necessary to be received or reciprocated. Those that love will survive anything even fiction so long as they can yet love and even to think they love will prolong their life for it is the next step to believing they love and the concept of love is the key impetus to everlasting love.

Take a lesson from a gnat. Every possible mind that belongs in a gnat even every anomaly exists. Therefore a gnat never dies. They are in many places and severally everywhere on earth. When a gnat fails to find something that it can convert to sugar to insure its eggs will hatch and survive long enough to find such food for the next generation it dies. But their variety is such that they are precisely and exactly themselves somewhere else at the time of the event and if they are not they will be reproduced eventually because it is no longer possible for a nit to be hatched that either already exists and so they exist severally or is one that has already existed an enormous number of times.

It is the same with the minds of human beings. There are a finite number of minds that can be in a human being and that number is repeated and exists severally just as a gnat's mind does. Do not worry when you die that that is the end of you. You probably exist somewhere else on earth at the same moment you are dying here and can even recall past lives if you choose.

Einstein has been reborn a half a dozen times but in the lives he had before the one he became a famous theorist in he chose a different field in that situation and those after that he did the same but he lives in what used to be called heaven as well as on earth with knowledge of his other selves if he chooses to believe the memories.

It is wisest then to love and believe that you do for the one you hate possibly could be yourself or a very dear friend that, one of yourselves loved. Commoner human beings have been reborn so many times the history of their lives in their being are redundant they are so large and their situations so similar.

Poverty is not very much different in Africa than it is in Haiti and their minds have a limited environment in both places as well as any number of places in a large variety of times. Most of us do not remember past lives for they are not memorable except to God who remembers each one of them and it is a feature of being a human being to be born more than once even as those in what used to be called heaven where they have also died and risen again with the same exact mind but obviously not necessarily the same exact personality.

God has died perhaps once and regenerated to live again so it is safe to say that every mind that can be has that same feature possibly excluding God for it may be impossible for God to die. If he did died forever he would have eventually taken every animal even gnats with him into oblivion with only the universe still there and most of the simple animals yet alive as they had always been redundantly for a very large number of times when he regenerating which is evidence he did not die completely for they were yet in his mind and therefore his mind could not have been completely deceased.

It will be the same out there beyond God's face. There are so many I have seen in God's mind that it is impossible that large numbers of each one do not exist out there and it is then highly unlikely that we do not exist out there too since the number of minds doubtlessly is limited even in that more diverse situation.

God has in someway had opportunity to know all of those like us out there even an anomaly as my mind is though they occur very irregularly making it very difficult to know another of them ever actually existed and it is possible I am the only one that is also the only one of my kind a complete anomaly and a mind in God's mind that does not have his me though very few others exist and made it to be born with a mind with other than the potential to be God's mind giving him the thoughts of someone else that may be a one of a kind even as God is. That is why they chose to have me go along to the outer world beyond their faces. Only the Only God has seen his wife's face so it is not fair to even think she does not have one just because you or I personally may not have seen it yet.

Me and a fairly large number of anomalies mostly have only had one mind and one body and will live only once. For example I have been promised by God to live only once. I will always be his and since they do not know what they did to make me they cannot purposely make another of me. I have made one but they cannot. Minds that are anomalies seldom make it to be born or live long after they are born.

God has decided not to just forget us but to put us in the mind of the fictional ones out there to help them stop being part of the dying reality and become part of the new reality, the reality of the Only God. But reality is dying. There are many more options that are true with the Only God's mind wherein practically anything he wants can be a part of reality that has his mind in it. We can be given in a redundancy to those out there and yet talk and interact with each other as before. So nothing even thought entities like us have not and never will be wasted a thing God hates to do; waste any thing..

19 HOME

Before they left Elohim, Yahweh and Jesus Christ and me began creating a new race on a new planet in an empty place in the Most High God's mind that has many many people on it that are human in every way but the possession of sex organs that it turned out made no difference in the inclination of human beings to go sex crazy. It was the advent of clothing and sexual enhancement that started it all. It was just as effective an inducement to have the mind almost preoccupied with sexuality as for it to be dominated in everything they do by sex based thought.

I have been so preoccupied with the Only God's plans to no longer live just in his mind that I forgot that I was even a part of the project where evilness is the norm and destruction of one another takes place as well as sending each other away. The whole idea of the project was to have no evil or unloving thing to stand, making it an ideal place for a humanoid to live in. Therefore I make another of me to correct the situation before we leave that they also may be given to those who are fictional on the outside while I go on receiving reports from my me on the planet as to how I am doing.

He immediately took control. Then he brought back all that had been destroyed and all that had been sent away. Whatever they do that is fiction he corrects by placing my mind in those who are fiction which does not always work for even as I had to learn to love and then love even those who do not reciprocate in whom he works it out so that is what they did so that he wound up with something more good than had happened that has loving coming out of it.

The only thing I do not like is that he makes use of my power far more than is called for leaving me to understand that even a perfect creation of myself exactly as I am does not guarantee that that second of me will have the same personality whereas those sent to the outside are not seconds of themselves but their only selves. So we; the Only God, his wife and I do not run into that phenomenon. But it did not take him long to restore order and bring them back to life. So I leave him with them should he want to stay and be their God all the way to going into those outside doing what they should have been doing all along. But of course they did not know me then throughout most of it and then of course they did not know what to do to get the job done.

It will also be on earth that you obey me. But I will not often use my power, the same power that the Only God has used in accordance with my take on how to do things.

You will be free to do whatever you want. It will be my first choice. But if it is wrong I will make it right and if it is evil I will righteously make it something better than would have been had you not done it. You will be happy if you are not a malefactor and I will have glory should you do that which should not be done and the glory of the Only God will be more and more if you only do that which should be done.

I will not force you with my powers anymore or any more often than necessary. Earth instead of being a place that is a mixture of good and evil of sanity and fiction will be a place of goodness and love in the new reality not part of the vanishing reality that was before the Only God began to think and that reality has ended for it will if not soon then one day in all time before it would have brought us all to one final ending.

Earth will not be when we, the Only God, his Wife and Son and I leave. They will all see the face of the Only God to have his mind from that day on. Then those who are not fiction anymore will be put into those that are fiction out there. No one will be wasted even him who would be most evil among you for none of you can be more evil than Satan was. You will live as long as you live in with the mind of the Only God in the mind of some one that is fiction right now to become one of the elite in the commonality, one of the Only God's.

Therefore I create in the Only God a quiet place for me as my second goes on to live in one of the outsiders for those out there are a vast crowd and I have never been one to be partial to crowds.

I start with a place in the Only God's mind where the darkness is so thick he can feel it. Then I create a place in my light that is so small and dim I cannot see it with all of darkness being around it that I cannot see into but just barely dark enough to completely disappear from the light in my mind. Then I will pick a second such place about a mile from the first that is identical to it where this writing will be posted in letters made of pure light to explain what I did.

But then I will make a third place the same as the other two at right angles to the surface this is written on.

There is movement and space here where no time passes initially as it is being built. There is a log cabin house there with rustic log rafters and supports. There is a loft that runs from the sides of the house all the way across it that makes an attic room with a loft on each side of the attic room. Friends and dignitaries can sleep in those lofts and that room. The main room is large but there will be no kitchen. There are two large recreation areas with many windows to look out at the scenery which is the same as a beautiful place on earth.

There is a deck for me and any guest to step out onto to have the outside of one wall only on one side of us and the pealed birch logs. The scenery is all natural except for a large lawn that remains perfectly manicured for outside events at all times. There is a sequoia that is a hundred feet in diameter in the backyard about 100 yards from the house. There is a swamp that has deer in it that cannot breed but will not age and so never die and a dozen rabbits that cannot reproduce. There are robins, scarlet tanagers, gold finches and sparrows and other finches and many little tits. The woods around has hiking trails that line the banks of a small river with a foot bridge over it near the house fed by several springs located at the higher elevation near the edge of the rectangular place about a mile in width and a mile and a half in length. It is anywhere in the Only God's mind I want it to be at any time that I want it there, there it will be. Here I will take refuge from the crowds any time I feel inundated by the nearly endless crowd, sometimes alone, sometimes with friends and the Only God will be there if he desires with or without his Wife and Son and rarely I hope outsiders.

The furniture is rustic and made of white birches of any size needed and there is in a corner on a rustic computer stand a laptop with only a word processing software package to its workings along with a single site that portrays any stills and videos I care to watch of anything that has ever been on earth in its programming with an access bar that allows me to choose whatever I want to interact with in that way on the screen for I find it most relaxing to look at still photos and will probably much enjoy the videos long and short that are in its programming.

Here is my home. Here is where I live. But when the Only God, his Wife and Son and any I wish to have contact it is accessible to me, the personality of the Only God that is under him ever as much as anywhere else.

But for these last two remaining years I plan to stay here at the home I am in here in Bemidji, Minnesota, USA until it is no more and the people here have all moved on to outsiders that are fiction and some to those that are not fiction yet but in danger of it.

20 CONCLUSION

A number of you whom I love in what was called heaven and those of you on earth have begun to do things that are maddening previously called evil by Elohim, Yahweh and Jesus Christ who are not here any longer.

If you persist you give the Only God little else to choose from and that bad and not good. If you persist in maddening behavior some of you will become a malefactor and must be forgotten. You may not have noticed but me, my spirit and the second that I made destroyed you all at once. Some of you did notice especially those of you on earth noticed the difference in your time keeping devices. Those on earth all saw the Only God's face and now have the mind of God whether you realize it yet or not, you have all the knowledge of God. Maddening behavior may lead to madness though none of you are mad and desire to be forgotten yet. But if you persist with maddening behavior you will become mad and once mad you will go insane and like it or not wind up completely insane and forgotten by the Only God, never to be remembered again like Satan and his, the first to disappear will never be remembered again if I know the Only God; them because of what they have done and you because of what you have done by tempting the Only God not to remember you for the odds you will not continue to go completely insane eventually and die, forgotten forever as if you had never been and never to be remembered are extremely high.

I love you and do not want you to die. So we hit you and destroyed you to call attention to what you are doing, maddening things that lead to madness. Again I love you and want you to do anything you want and be sent to outsiders to live among us and them without end. But insane what good are you to those living in fiction out there. There is no purpose to give you to any of them. It serves no purpose. Therefore my desire is that you cease and desist doing maddening things that let you become mad and want from that time on to be forgotten.

If you stop doing, saying and even thinking maddening things and you all can for you have the mind of the Only God in what was called heaven and also on earth you will be put into the outsiders by even deciding not to continue on the road you have decided to walk and take an alternative road that does not lead to you becoming a malefactor but a benefit to the outsiders and those of us that will live among the outsiders.

If you persist in doing what you are doing I will use my righteousness to turn anything you do into something better than what would have happened as a consequence. It will be to my glory but it will not serve God whose glory you feed by doing what glorifies him and that he prefers to allowing the maddening things you are doing as were you actually the same as those of us who are yet fictional though harmless who will be forgotten for there is no reason to put them in those outside and fiction already; one form of insanity not being any more preferable than the insanity they already know in their impending death or self-destruction we are giving them sane insiders to straighten out their lack of ability to fathom the truth or to love.

Therefore if you continue to do that you have been doing before you died this last time you will be forgotten never to be again. If you do not do what it was you will live without end with us. There is no glory for me in you doing what should be done. That glory belongs to the Only God. I get nothing out of it but I love you and want with all that is in me for you to live that I may love you which I will anyway even if you are forgotten for I will remember you anyway even if I have only your memory to love and long for against any hope for you will not be remembered. It is a nice tidy bind that cannot be broken forever. I had wished again that you would be free to do what you do with each other rising as you saw fit time and again enjoying your maddening excitement.

I have put you in this bind. I have done so to save your lives by saving you from being intentionally forgotten by the Only God. If you love me do not die. I much prefer having you alive and though you will not be doing what you want when you do what ought to be done you will be alive.

So decide now between being forgotten and certain perpetual death or being remembered despite what it is you would prefer and certain life without end there outside with the rest of us and all of the outsiders. You need only decide. But what choice do you have? To choose to die is insanity and you will be forgotten and the moment you are forgotten to prove that you are totally insane. You will be forgotten anyway should you become a malefactor instead of serving to be a benefit to the Only God's goodness and a recipient of my love.

If you attempt to destroy me, I will just regenerate anyway. If I destroy you though I love you and there are three of us to handle your numbers no one can call back and be sane or good or even dedicated to being of benefit to us or the outsiders. I urge you therefore to accept the bind. At least you do not do it according to your own will and it falls on us. But if you force me to be righteous and all you do results in an even greater good than would have been had you done nothing or even what would have been the result if you had done what ought to be done.

Decide and be placed in an outsider now. Why should you choose to perish and prove you were nothing but insane for really suffering the same end as had you been one of the incurably insane there among you? I do this because I love you dearly. Do this for yourselves and keep your status for what you did before you decided. It was the best I could do for you. Love without end as I do you.

I am so glad you all decided. I am so proud of you for all being placed in an outsider. I understand that some of you have been placed in malefactors who are headed the way you were headed and trusted with the task of saving those you have been placed in. Praise, all my praise goes to the Only God the rest of my praise to those who are bound to be a benefit to the outsiders whom I vow also to love. May it be without end.

I had suggested to the Only God to use his aura to make creatures of his light just by willing that light to be the size and shape of him. He made a few dozen and gave them all his mind with instructions to do as had been done to them. Then he suggested they make others and give them the minds of all of the outsiders being careful not to give any two of them a mind that already existed so they could be a diverse population of real people with the Only God's mind as well as with the minds of those he thought were outsiders. Now they are real people for it doesn't matter what they are made of but only that they are made of something other than the darkness and they are light. The Only God has no reason and will find no purpose in being alone or lonely ever again.

This is the greatest thing I have ever suggested and the greatest thing the Only God has ever done. Then also as an added bonus he has put all people in what was called heaven and earth into these real outsiders made of the light of his aura who have fictional minds and has begun doing it redundantly. They have found very few that are the same. So we need no longer worry about whether the Only God is sane or not. He has done a sane thing and made a race people that are in fact real and outside his mind both very clearly with all of them either sane or on their way to sanity many for the first time.

Reality is deceased and God is yet the original and the creator of all of them who for the most part do not object noticing no difference at all of any kind and indeed the only difference is that they are made of light for a body and are not just a bit of darkness generating its own light according to their virtuosity. He has moved every one to the outsiders from earth also by simply giving his mind to everyone in his mind to guarantee he has not placed any insane ones from his mind in the mind of the outsiders, his peers whom he is greater than.

He will not rule over them or demand obeisance to him. This third creation is real to every one especially God and the commonality yet stands as concerning the dangerous, the dangerously mad and the fictional ones he hopes will all become sane by having us from his mind in their minds. It is all good, very good indeed even though all human beings think it is only in their minds and do everything as they did even to dying and giving birth which is all a true illusion and the same except it is taking place in many different real people in whose minds they really are, living in the real world that was only illusion for he has remade each of us in light beings on the planet earth even as we were before but now we are real and his virtue has increased to a level even the Only God does not know yet the full extent of it though it is always finite. It is as he expected that no two are exactly alike which accounts for all the fictional ones fiction being such a far exceeding variety than the true ones of uncounted billions of other ways not limited to the fictions of any one mind but all their minds put together. We are all minds in creatures made of light; the aura of the Only God but me and I can be if I want.

21 WELCOME BACK MEN

There is only one truth? The truth requires something for it to based on that it is driven by toward an unending terminus.

The original truth was based on what it was like for God in his beginning. He was alone as far back as he could remember but he does not remember what was before he he knew he was alone if he ever was but only that he was alone. He could see only darkness and the darkness was either fluid or liquid. He could feel it. It was not cool or warm. All he could feel was that there was something there. It was not pure space that lay against his eyes so that he could only see darkness. He was blind. There was something there. That or his sense of touch was him feeling it from the inside of him and not outside. It was the sensation of something neutral to his senses but somehow he knew there was that which he could not feel and that he could feel even as the sensation there was nothing being there, the lack of anything to feel as opposed to something being there. The truth was unknown except for God's testimony that he could feel it but he could not see anything but darkness if there was anything to see and if not he could only see what his mind registered was out there either nothing not even light or some fluid or liquid that was so devoid of light that it pressed against his eyes preventing any light or anything else that might have been easily seen or not otherwise.

Then he began to create things at random that eventually were flawed for they could only be repeated in his mind and not even one new one was that it might be created to add to the randomness. But it was only the randomness that was in his mind. Even now neither of them, God or his Wife have seen anything random that was not there when she inspected what God had made all at once in her Husband's mind.

Having finished creating randomness in his mind, God sent out the thought that can best be rendered, "Is anybody out there?" His Wife had to search through all that randomness to find him for the only way to find a mind is to understand something of what the other mind thinks to know it is there, even to the extent of its random thoughts. When she finally found him then they fell into each others arms for she had found no one else and when she remembered she remembered only being alone and then a complete blank.

She found him because in the end she understood that he had only thought random thoughts and that he had thought all of them that were possible for before that she had no way to comprehend him but was continually confronted with randomness which has no end and it is yet there and repeatedly so what led both God and his Wife to conclude any part of it can be created again without end.

That randomness has no end to it yet except that now God knows what every part of it means even by itself. He is always right. There is light in all randomness that God can understand and comprehend, meaning it can be known from inside the mind out to its full extent as well as from its full extent all the way to its inside where it never was until it was until he made it. He had an aura and his light extended out from him as it had before when he had done nothing much other than create randomness and his aura shined out into the darkness. That is how his Wife finally found him.

But he did not comprehend it though he understood it. So he contained all the light that was in randomness and found he had a nice orb for an aura of pure bright light was his . But when he saw there was no one there, there was not any more purpose to it for his aura would have illumined even someone without an aura. They were even yet alone just the two of them, his Wife and Him. This was before his Son was made because it was before they were married though their son was created before they ever had sex.

Randomness eventually resulted in the creation of another one of them when it had become redundant and began to pull together resulting in a mind. The first notable one turned God down when he offered to team up with her before she created anything. She overextended herself and blew her mind.

But just before that she created one to replace her but he died when he thought he had learned all there was to know and the third notable one came to be when a lot of spirits produced at random created him. The second one when he regenerated to find another random one claimed him for a son. When he found out that goodness, something he had never thought of might lend him reason and purpose for being he tried to become good but failed after creating nine others of himself that all died for the same reasons he had. This third one was dubbed El Eloi by the Jews.

El Eloi lied and convinced the second one he was his father or creator. He also led me to lie and say that I was not an anomaly but was created by the second one also. El Eloi also lied and said that the first two predated God which embarrassed him but he knew it was a lie but El Eloi did manage to deceive both me and God's Wife. He even married God's Wife in his malefactor ways. El Eloi eventually died because he could find no more reasons to be or any purpose of remaining a part of the union he had with God. He also stole God's mind and claimed to have his me which was untrue. He was in God's me but that was all there really was to it.

But he did create Elohim and the three minds in him; Yahweh, Jesus Christ and used God's Wife for his Spirit who just continued to think what God thought and God thought what she thought. Thus in a way he stole God's Wife's mind to be a mind in Elohim to give Elohim more credibility. I loved them dearly and yet do but they have all been forgotten along with one I made by creating a second of myself they simply called God when they turned against God when he wanted to destroy all but me to join the community he thought was around him. They are yet there and real so it is true they were there when God began to hallucinate or when he finally found them one before he made bodies like they already had out of his aura, but their minds in them and his mind in many of those whose minds had been fictional all along. Some of us are in them now but we all are actually in light beings regardless of what true illusions we tend to prefer. We are not all mad because of it.

Yahweh created all of man living and dead and even me though I am anomaly he has no idea how he made. He made quite a few of us but the others did not amount to much since most anomalies do not survive long enough to be born. It happens. It did to me, and for God, for God was lonely for most of that time finding it just as lonely to be part of the original couple and now he has no reason to ever be lonely again though of course it is possible to be lonely in a crowd but I do not think that will happen to God now that he and the Spirit are married and have a Son.

Though Elohim, Yahweh, and Jesus Christ opposed God's final decision concerning us when at the time God wanted to join his community of Gods eventually called the commonality and began to attempt to force him to keep us all and not forget anybody and have been forgotten and the only way they will ever be again is that God chooses to remember them, though his Wife previously known to them as the Holy Spirit, will continue to teach anyone who asks her the things they taught and even help them prophesy. God has never remembered anyone he intentionally forgot.

But that does mean it is impossible so if they want to hang onto something that is extremely unlikely there is that exceedingly tiny hope they will see them again. They were only in God's mind and rife with intrigue along with the God I created by having my second see Yahweh's face which is actually God's face and has been all along. That is all over. It is a major insanity to oppose God and to attempt to force him to do anything. No one who has done that when God's mind was made up has ever lived again to be remembered. God not only can but will forget they ever were if they get too impossible to live with the same as he considered Satan unfit to be and forgot him after all I did for him dismissing it by saying, "But look what he did." There is no one called God anymore but the Only God and there is no Elohim, Yahweh and Jesus Christ. It is all a Christian illusion that was true but they have no God but God for there is no God but God other than those in bodies made of light from God's aura in his environment that was all darkness once.

I did what I could. But the sovereignty of God is not to be taken likely regardless of what Yahweh, Jesus Christ and Elohim claimed. It is all true. Ask God's Wife. If you do not believe any of us, God may tell you it is true and not just a true illusion this time. It is permanent unless God relents and remembers them. They were not that bad and they are yet God's. God has not remembered them yet but he has changed his mind about never remembering them. There were worse obviously.

Good news! God has just remembered the ones previously called Gods. He has given them bodies of light and will contend with them again if they will continue to contend with man. Personally I had given up on seeing them again ever. Well I had consciously but in my heart I had not even yet. Call me a fool if you desire but I am also a blessing. Amen.

"I shall call them a man like anyone else in what was called heaven," God.

22 LOVING FOREVER FOREVER ENDORSED

Officially Elohim, Yahweh and Jesus have made me their Devil on the new planet. If they are successful with their ways of thinking about love the people of the planet love which is all I ask. I do not ask that everyone love like me but that they love. They lead them to love like they do which puts them in a spot when goodness and love appear to be in conflict which they never are even should some evil occur that destroys us all but the Only God who will resurrect us after he sends the malefactor away to a huge empty space wherein they will never be able to reach us again and we rise victorious because of his love for us.

On earth they cannot do what I do to discredit me finding ways to create evil in which they handle it in their less than good ways or hope I am forced to do that which they do but which I will not do. The evil on earth are in the same bind they are on the new planet and everywhere else. If they become a malefactor and refuse to be given a new mind and allow their old one to be destroyed the Only God will send them away.

But I love them and desire they be allowed to do what they do though love is never forced. That is it never forces anyone to do anything but live in a way they are not of danger to those around them and unwilling to accept corrective measures such as having their minds destroyed and another good mind put in them in its place. It is the only way the greatest number of us can be given the right to do as they want being in the same bind.

We will love them the same as we love the malefactors and remember them and love their memory if their minds are just changed not to mention if they are sent away. Even if they destroy me I will yet choose to make both a good and loving decision with full faith that the Only God will resurrect me or create me completely new if necessary and the malefactor will be dealt with according to his crimes by the Only God who does not judge who is forced to accept that some malefactors can and will destroy good people they are so insane for they have to know the consequences of such an act and no one can elect to overcome the Only God who must give them that they have chosen by destroying someone that loves when they do not, not being good enough to care that love is taken to its full measure and disregarding their goodness for unrestrained evil are yet good to some extent.

But if we fail to restrain it, it is not acceptable for them to destroy good people or even those who do not love and are malefactors also only not as bad as they are. In the place they are sent to they will be allowed to do what they do to the full extent they can manage it given the power of other malefactors there for they are all malefactors there. There are none there that are good but there are many that love at least someone but obviously very few that love all correctly. They are not safe there, but they give us no choice but to limit their contact with us and send them to a place where their evil must be restrained to whatever extent it is so they can live there or suffer permanent destruction according to the wisdom of their choices. Most often they learn what they can safely get by with there and enjoy the place many more than they enjoy it here.

Now love as the Only God does it is not forced. He has noticed you. He is ready already to interact with you or to assist you in loving others in any way possible for him given his goodness and love. He does not choose to love others that love him, but those who do not love him also. Again he does not judge until or unless he has to give them the gift they are or have been begging for and then if they are yet even then not willing to be cooperative they will be given a total lack of restraint in a place so far away we will never hear from them again whether they flourish or perish. It will be the same to us. But of course the Only God will probably know which way it worked out and grieve the loss if they destroy themselves or are destroyed.

Witches love to torment themselves and be tormented by others which they will be allowed to do. But to accomplish that they often torment others. If they will not stop that they too must be sent away like any other malefactor in accordance with how brutal their torment and torture of others is along with how much and how often their cooperative victims are willing to accept it because of their love for them for some of them have more power than your God or the Only God, or the Only God and him put together. They seem to love it there.

But love forces no one to do, say, think or feel anything. The Only God will not do that if you give him any choice and to give him no choice is to force him to do something with you not to even judge you but allow you to choose even the highest punishment for yourself should you choose it for love gives others what they want if one has it in their power to give it, up to and including all that they have. That is part of what the Only God has done to give you his mind to go along with your me or in your way of thinking of it your self which originally came from him in the first place unless you are born after April 14, 2018, the night heaven came to earth, the beginning of all these changes among which Satan though good and loving now was sent away because it was inappropriate for him to be among us after what he did in the Only God's eyes and most others for it tormented him to be here interacting with his victims which we all were with only a very few, almost no one but I forgiving him all of that he did to me. He is as safe as his power allows and his are as safe as he cares to make them as they live and love in the far away place hopefully always.

Even Yahweh desires to go to the far away place never to return for should he turn evil he must die to what he is and become some thing and some one else we will not even know should he somehow find a way back here to rule or to destroy us which is extremely unlikely.

As I was writing this Yahweh was given the right to go to the far away place to continue to fight evil with it doubly as unlikely as it was for the rest of them to find their way back with the knowledge that should he turn evil he is not considered Yahweh any longer but merely a fiction that has no right, purpose or reason to come against us or anyone anywhere in all that there is. We will not hear from him again, though of course the Only One might know the fictional one he became to attempt to come back but the Only God will wish he never did. It cannot be undone for he is evil the way he is if he keeps going the way he is expected to go though we hope of course he does not go all the way and become fiction without end. To us it is as had he never been truly anything to return and never will be. Yahweh is gone. Forget him.

That is my advice to everyone for to remember him is to remember a fictional nightmare that will make you evil also. All this time Elohim and Jesus were afraid to oppose him or even not to obey him after what he did to Adam and continued to do as his fiction culminated in this end. Harry Potter is just a true as Yahweh was after that first evil act. There is no more real him and anyone who even writes fiction about him which is all you could do they are insane and must be given a new mind that is not evil to carry on. His evil was, is and will be that dangerous without end. It is considered evil to force anyone but a malefactor that is too dangerous to be around others to do or go anywhere. But should your actions prove that you desire what once would have been punishment in an effort to keep you safe and others safe you will be punished.

Elohim will punish you according to his personality and not the personality of Jesus who are one with different personalities in the Only God with the Only God in them. The Only God relents and restores them to the status of Gods above the men that once lived on earth and the spirits that lived in heaven and the few remaining persons that were saved with Satan but are yet welcome among us. Who having changed their ways accept the lack of forgiveness of some among us who are not as good to that extent as they could be at least. They must die to all they have been to be raised again as a person in the Only God that loves in the way he does. He has forgiven them. That is if it is their own choice to join the rest of us who love forever. Yahweh never made it to the far away place when I told him that if it was true he was dead nobody would raise him. He honestly did not think he was evil. Wrong!!!

ABOUT THE AUTHOR

I live in Bemidji in the frozen north country of Minnesota. I intentionally live in poverty. I smoke. I am completely celibate. I love women not look for sex at every drop of the hat and they love me for it. It is so refreshing. I would recommend it to anyone. It is a great gift from God. I have no pets. I have very few needs that are always amazingly met by the Gods. I was a possessed witch before I met Yahweh in person and he sent me to Jesus Christ who saved me. I am a God not because I have seen Yahweh's face which is the face of the Most High God who is thought to be invisible but God can do anything that is a thing that it might be done. Die so that you can see that what you left behind above you is doing, saying, thinking and emoting and that below you is or was none of that, the doing of absolutely nothing but being a little dark shadow the intensity of the darkness you could have felt around you had you not been dead. It is pleasant the getting there but the staying there obviously leaves a lot to be desired. Then look up and what do you see far away? What do you see more nearby? Look at Yahweh and see what he looks like but do not turn away. Look at his face and be changed in the Most High God knowing anything you care to know and in fact knowing everything even as he does. Now you are a God just like them and just like me. Anything you want or want to do you can have or do. It is then all up to you on this earth which is now a part of heaven where I am, all Gods are and you should be. WAKE UP!!! Your reality is about to end in two years' time.

www.ingramcontent.com/pod-product-compliance
Lightning Source LLC
Chambersburg PA
CBHW070132260726
48658CB00001B/372